PUB WALKS

The Midshires Way

TWENTY CIRCULAR WALKS IN
BUCKINGHAMSHIRE & NORTHAMPTONSHIRE

James A. Lyons

COUNTRYSIDE BOOKS

NEWBURY, BERKSHIRE

First Published 1995
© James A Lyons 1995

COUNTRYSIDE BOOKS
3 Catherine Road
Newbury, Berkshire

ISBN 1 85306 323 1

This one's for Siggy

Designed by Mon Mohan
Cover illustration by Colin Doggett
Photographs by the author
Maps by S. R. Lyons

Produced through MRM Associates Ltd., Reading
Typeset by The Midlands Book Typesetting Company, Loughborough
Printed and bound by Woolnough Bookbinding Ltd., Irthlingborough

Contents

Publisher's Note

We hope that you obtain considerable enjoyment from this book; great care has been taken in its preparation. However, changes of landlord and actual closures are sadly not uncommon. Likewise, although at the time of publication all routes followed public rights of way or permitted paths, diversion orders can be made and permissions withdrawn.

We cannot of course be held responsible for such diversion orders and any inaccuracies in the text which result from these or any other changes to the routes nor any damage which might result from walkers trespassing on private property. However we are anxious that all details covering the walks and the pubs are kept up to date and would therefore welcome information from readers which would be relevant to future editions.

Introduction

This is the first in a new series entitled *Pub Walks along* ... which builds on the success of the existing *Pub Walks* in each county by using middle and long-distance paths as a different basis for circular pub walks. In addition to acting as a guide to pubs along the way, each book provides an ideal introduction to the long-distance path by incorporating sections of it in circular walks that are full of interest and yet generally undemanding. Completion of them all is, of course, by no means essential to the enjoyment of the individual walks but would make an interesting challenge, at the end of which you might be tempted to say, 'Done that, been there' - and with some routes planned for the future, you may even be able to buy the T-shirt!

As a new path in the long-distance network the Midshires Way was chosen to launch the series because it provides a hitherto 'missing link' down the centre of England between the long-distance footpaths in the north and those in the south. Opened in August 1994, it travels north from the Chilterns for over 200 miles to connect with the Trans Pennine walk from Manchester, and in so doing incorporates a variety of rights of way through the counties of Buckinghamshire, Northamptonshire, Leicestershire, Derbyshire and into Greater Manchester. Each county has produced a map plus information relating to the linear route within its boundaries which can be purchased separately, or in a combined pack, from any of the local authorities whose joint efforts have led to the successful creation of this route.

For the purposes of this book the overall route has been divided into a northern and southern half, the latter consisting of *Pub Walks along The Midshires Way* in the two counties of Buckinghamshire and Northamptonshire. My thanks are due to the Leisure Services Departments of both counties for their co-operation and advice relating to the rights of way incorporated in the pub walks.

A double-acorn logo is used for waymarking throughout the entire length of the Midshires Way. It symbolises the way in which the route links two National Trails, the Ridgeway and the Trans Pennine, which, like all such trails, are waymarked with single acorns. The Midshires Way was itself created by linking existing rights of way and/or middle-distance routes and this is shown by the way in which the double-acorn logo has been added to existing waymarking. The Midshires Way was planned for multi-purpose use by horse-riders, cyclists and walkers and for long stretches a common route is followed. However, where the walkers' diverges from the riders' route, then it is the walkers' route that is followed in this book.

In Buckinghamshire the Midshires Way is over 40 miles long and travels north, from the Chilterns, to Salcey Forest in Northamptonshire. Two well established routes are used: the North Bucks Way for walkers, and the Swan's Way for walkers and riders. The North Bucks Way is indicated along its route by labelled discs, the Swan's Way by the distinctive logo of a swan's head and horseshoe. In relation to the Midshires Way, both these routes have different starting points and diverge from time to time as they head north. However, through Milton Keynes and up to the Northamptonshire border, the route stays with the Swan's Way. In this county, waymarking for rights of way not referred to above consists of green metal fingerposts, plus white discs with a yellow arrow for footpaths, blue for bridleways. For further information, contact the Planning and Transportation Department, County Hall, Aylesbury, Bucks HP20 1UY. Tel: 01296 395000.

In Northamptonshire a common route consisting of tracks and minor roads is followed as far as Blisworth. Here, walkers diverge to follow the towpath of the Grand Union canal as far as Nether Heyford, above which the walking and riding routes diverge twice for short distances before reaching the Brampton Valley Way. Walkers continue north along this dismantled railway as far as Great Oxendon, beyond which the route coincides with this county's latest long-distance footpath, the Jurassic Way (black arrow with white fossil shell logo on white disc). The combined routes travel east for a few miles before parting and rejoining to cross over the Leicestershire border. In this part of the county waymarking generally consists of fingerposts with white lettering or white discs with black arrows. For further information contact Northamptonshire Countryside Centre. Tel: 01604 237220.

This book combines information on the long-distance route, including any accommodation, with a detailed description of ten pubs and circular walks in each county. Pubs which have been selected are as close to the line of the route as possible and offer a warm welcome, real ale and homecooking. As such they range from village 'locals' to city 'watering-holes', from canal-side pubs to country inns. Pubs, in short, to suit all tastes, combined with walks to suit all levels of ability and interests.

The circular walks from each pub vary in length from 2½ miles to 6 miles and cover attractive countryside in the two counties. In addition, each pub walk incorporates a stretch of the Midshires Way which, in this book, is covered at intervals from the Chilterns in Buckinghamshire, to the Leicestershire border. The basis of organisation is, therefore, flexible enough not only to provide a guide to the 20 pubs and pub walks along the way, but also to act as a general guide to the overall route. Those undertaking the entire long-distance route will also need the information pack from the local authorities referred to above. Those walking the pub walks need only stout shoes or boots and a copy of this book!

But whichever you are undertaking, please remember that the sketch maps in the book are designed as simple guides for the starting points of the walks and they provide an overall view of the routes. For those who wish to use detailed maps, the relevant Ordnance Survey Landranger map is recommended and is given in the preamble to each pub walk.

Finally, the preparation of this book was a team effort. My wife, Sally, drew the sketch maps and together we walked many miles to find the best available combination of pubs and walks. Here's wishing you every success with pub walks along the southern half of the Midshires Way – may you enjoy them and the countryside along this new long-distance route as much as we did!

James A. Lyons
Spring 1995

Key for strip maps

•••••••••••• Midshires Way

[1]   location of Pub Walk

Key for Pub Walk maps

•••••••••••• Midshires Way

➜ ➜ ➜   Pub Walk

➜•••➜••• Pub Walk incorporating Midshires Way

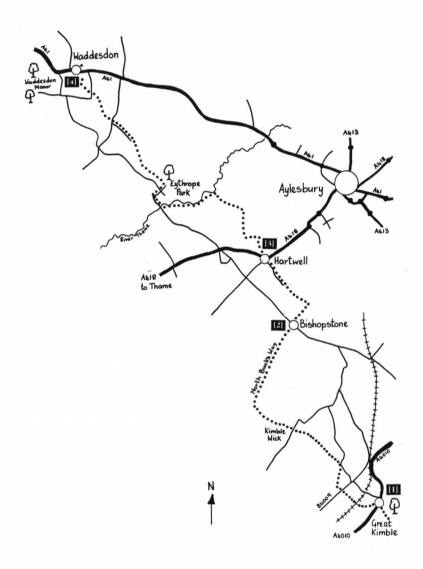

Map showing location of Pub Walks 1–4.

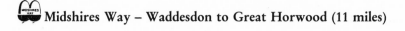

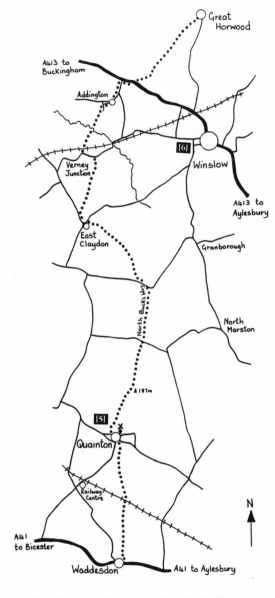

Map showing location of Pub Walks 5–6.

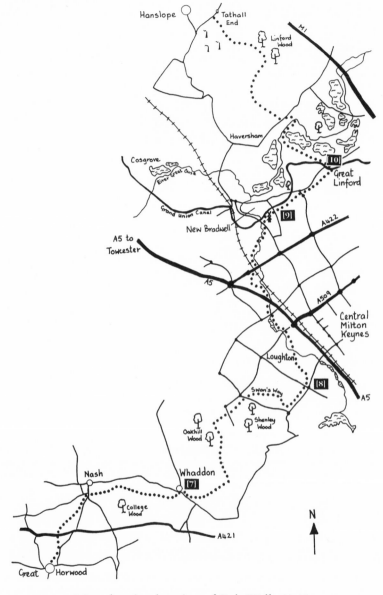

Map showing location of Pub Walks 7–10.

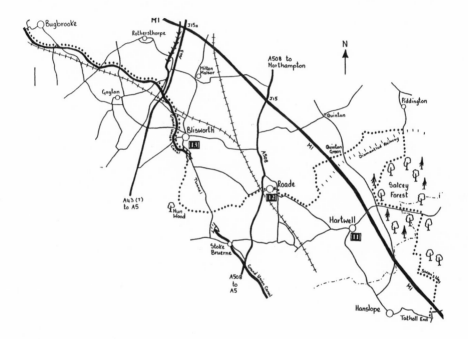

Map showing location of Pub Walks 11–13.

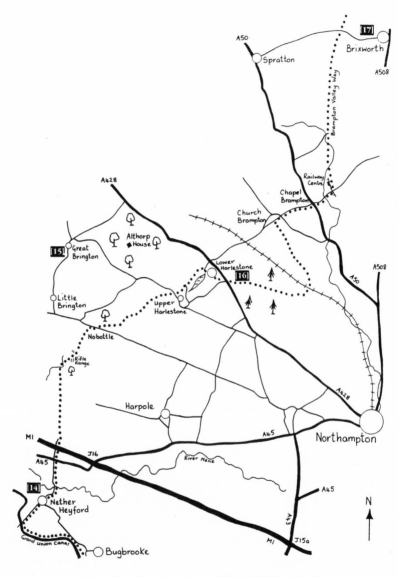

Map showing location of Pub Walks 14–17.

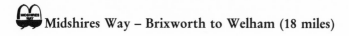

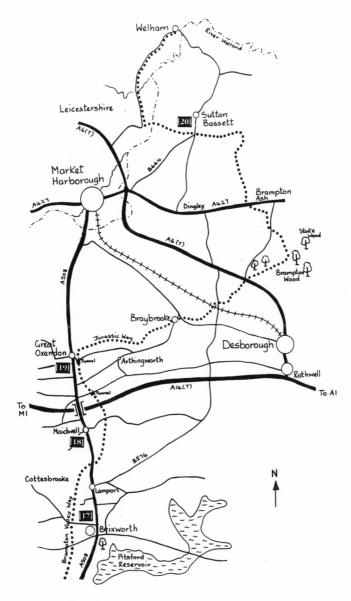

Map showing location of Pub Walks 18–20.

Midshires Way – Overall route from the Ridgeway to the Pennines.

[1] Great Kimble
The Bernard Arms

Great Kimble is of ancient origins and this area along the base of the Chilterns provides evidence of wider settlement in medieval times.

The Bernard Arms is on the main road, on the corner of Church Lane, opposite the church. A substantial building, it was altered and extended in the 1930s, a process which has continued to the present day. As an inn with accommodation, it makes an ideal starting point for the Midshires Way. It is also the closest pub to Chequers and has served some distinguished customers over the years – a photograph on display shows almost the entire population of the village waving goodbye to Harold Wilson the day he drank his last pint here.

The bar is very comfortable, whilst the general decor has small touches which reflect the influence of the pub's French landlord who has built up a reputation for high quality food and attention to detail. There is a very wide choice of home-cooked food, including a range of fish dishes such as the Mediterranean seafood mix, or lemon pepper catfish. Wherever possible dishes such as the loin of pork with sage sauce are prepared with herbs freshly picked from the garden. Meals are not served on Sunday nights. There is a separate games room, in which children are welcome, plus a very pleasant garden and children's play area to the rear of the pub.

In addition to a comprehensive wine list the landlord takes pride in the availability of well over 20 malt whiskies. Cask conditioned beers include Ind Coope Burton Ale, Benskins Best Bitter, Tetley Bitter and Wadworth 6X.

The opening times are Monday to Saturday from 11 am to 3 pm and 6 pm to 11 pm, and on Sunday from noon to 3 pm and 7 pm to 10.30 pm.

Telephone: 01844 346172/3.

How to get there: Great Kimble is about 4 miles south of Aylesbury, midway between Wendover and Princes Risborough. The pub is on the A4010, next to the church.

Parking: There is a large car park to one side of the pub.

Length of the walk: 5 miles (shorter option possible). Map: OS Landranger 165 Aylesbury and Leighton Buzzard (inn GR 825061).

A walk which incorporates a stretch of the Ridgeway National Trail, with fine views across Aylesbury Vale from the Chilterns, plus a closer view of Chequers, the Prime Minister's official country residence. A short stretch of the Midshires Way is included as an introduction to the long-distance route which runs from here to the Trans Pennine Way.

The Walk

From the pub the route turns right, down Church Lane. Past some attractive cottages it turns right again, just this side of a railway bridge. Down some steps the path continues ahead following the circular walk signs to the road. Here, the route turns left, past the railway station, where it crosses to the other side of the road to follow a roadside path.

After the Crown and Brookside Farm it turns right, still following the circular walk across mainly arable fields. Past a pond it turns left and, eventually, right, heading up rising ground towards Ellesborough church. To the left of the church a monument dedicated to the Buckinghamshire men who died in the Boer War stands out prominently on the line of the Chilterns. Up a steep bank the path leads into the churchyard where steps climb up to the church itself from where there are the first good views across Aylesbury Vale below. From the front of the church the path runs down a bank and the route crosses straight over a road.

(From here a short-cut can be taken by following the footpath to the right, although this route misses out Chequers.)

Having crossed the road, the main route continues ahead along a

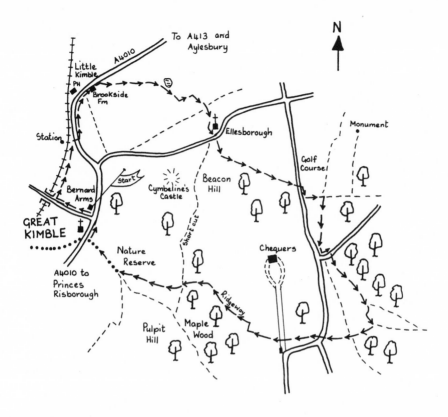

sunken track to just before a private property sign, where it turns left. The path runs down across a wide, arable field to the road where the route turns right, along the grass verge. After a short distance, it turns left on a track down the side of Combe Hill Farm to the lower slopes of the Chiltern Hills. At a Y-junction the route turns right, following the circular walk along the base of the hills through mixed woodland to the road. Here, the route turns left along the verge with the first glimpse of Chequers across the fields to the right. Within a few yards, it turns left, up a lane, and almost immediately right on a track behind a house. Here it takes the left-hand fork following the yellow arrow painted on the front of an ash tree. The path now runs through woodland that turns from mixed to predominantly beech and, eventually, the Ridgeway long-distance path with its single acorn waymark is joined. The route stays with the Ridgeway as it continues ahead across many other crossing paths on the flanks of the hills. Occasional clearings provide good downhill views through the trees and the path eventually leaves

17

the line of the hills as it crosses over the road to Chequers to follow a broad path across arable fields.

Over the fields the route passes through metal swing-gates either side of Victory Drive with its avenue of beech trees planted by Winston Churchill during his time as Prime Minister in the post-war era. Bearing in mind all the accomplishments and achievements of this great man and war-time leader of the nation, one can only wonder at the creative energy that found time for the planting of trees or, another practical skill in which he took great pride, the building of brick garden-walls at Chartwell, his real home in the country.

The path continues to follow the edge of Maple Wood, at the end of which a metal swing-gate gives access to an arable field. From here the path crosses to a second gate and over a track where the short-cut referred to earlier comes in from the right. This is a good spot to have a rest and enjoy the wide views before following the path ahead past a nature reserve below in the hollow of the combe on the right. The path bears left at the next fingerpost to a final swing-gate, where the route turns right and runs downhill on a good track.

On the right, a few yards down this sunken track, a prominent double-acorn waymark marks the official start of the Midshires Way and records overall mileage. From here the track continues downhill to a road which the long-distance route crosses straight over and heads north for distant Derbyshire.

The pub walk, however, turns right and follows the roadside path up the hill and back to the Bernard Arms.

Midshires Way – Great Kimble to Bishopstone (5 miles)

Having crossed the road at the bottom of the hill below the Bernard Arms (see above), the route follows the North Bucks Way across pastures and past Old Grange Farmhouse. It then turns right, crosses a single track railway and a road (Lower Icknield Way). Past Hollytree Farm a hedged track is followed to another road along which the route turns left. Down Kimblewick Farm drive it turns left at the second cattle grid, then right behind the farmhouse. A headland path continues across several fields to meet another metalled drive leading to the road into Kimble Wick. At a T-junction the route is joined by the Swan's Way which continues ahead on a stony track. Eventually, the track turns right and a headland path is followed. After some distance the Swan's Way leaves on the left, but the walker's route continues ahead along the North Bucks Way and is described in Pub Walk 2, from the Harrow, Bishopstone.

[2] Bishopstone
The Harrow

Situated in a quiet hamlet surrounded by farmland, the Harrow is appropriately named considering its rural location.

Originally built as a cottage in the 19th century, it remained thatched until the early 1900s when it was extended and re-roofed with tiles. Today, it is a good example of an unpretentious village pub and has built up a loyal and regular clientele by serving high quality, home-cooked pub grub and well kept beer. One bar serves a spacious, open plan area furnished with solid, wooden tables, a selection of chairs with comfortable cushions, and chunky stools. A log fire adds an extra touch of comfort to an already warm and hospitable welcome. In keeping with its serviceable and friendly image, generous portions of home-cooked food are available at very reasonable prices and dishes such as home-made lasagne and quiche keep the customers coming back for more. Summer favourites include chicken breast in lemon and coriander sauce or seafood platter. Winter warmers include chilli dishes or hearty servings of sausage and mash. In addition, blackboard specials provide a constant change of menu. Vegetarians are catered for and there is a children's menu. Hot meals are not available on Sunday nights, or on Mondays. There is a good sized garden and play area for children behind the pub. Dogs are not allowed in the bars.

The Harrow is a Pubmaster pub and cask beers on offer include Worthington Best Bitter and Draught Bass. Worthington Keg, Guinness, two lagers and cider are also available on draught.

The opening times are Monday to Saturday from 11.30 am to 2.30 pm, and 6 pm to 11 pm, and on Sunday from noon to 3 pm and 7 pm to 10.30 pm.

Telephone: 01296 748652.

How to get there: Bishopstone is just 2 miles south-west of Aylesbury. Turn off the A418 (Aylesbury to Thame) at Hartwell or Stone on a C road to Haddenham. The hamlet of Bishopstone, with the pub at its centre, is signposted at the first crossroads.

Parking: There is a large car park to one side of the pub.

Length of the walk: 3¹/₂ miles. Map: OS Landranger 165 Aylesbury and Leighton Buzzard (inn GR 803106).

A walk that explores rolling farmland typical of this area of Aylesbury Vale. From high ground which includes the site of an abandoned medieval village there are good views of the Chilterns to the south.

The Walk

From the Harrow, the route turns right and follows the road for a good distance. Past the thatched Old School House, it turns left, along the Swan's Way bridletrack. After passing some barns, it turns left again on a headland path which runs down to a hedge. Here, it turns right along to a short section of hedged track which leads to two metal gates each side of a footbridge. The walk continues ahead up the sloping pasture aiming to the left of a red-tiled barn at the far end. The mounds and hollows in this field are the only indications that a medieval village once stood here. Nothing is known for certain about why this particular village came to be abandoned, although many such rural villages were forcibly depopulated by land-owners in order to make more land available for sheep grazing. If this happened here, then nothing much has changed since, as sheep remain the only inhabitants of this lonely and deserted place.

A swing-gate to the left of the barn takes the path to a track which continues ahead, passing on the left the remains of the moat which once surrounded the old Manor House. Past the near derelict buildings of Moreton Farm the track arrives at a metal gate, beyond which the route continues as a headland path down the side of a wide, arable field. There are good views of the line of the Chilterns from here as this part of the walk is on relatively high ground, the nearby trig point being almost 300 ft

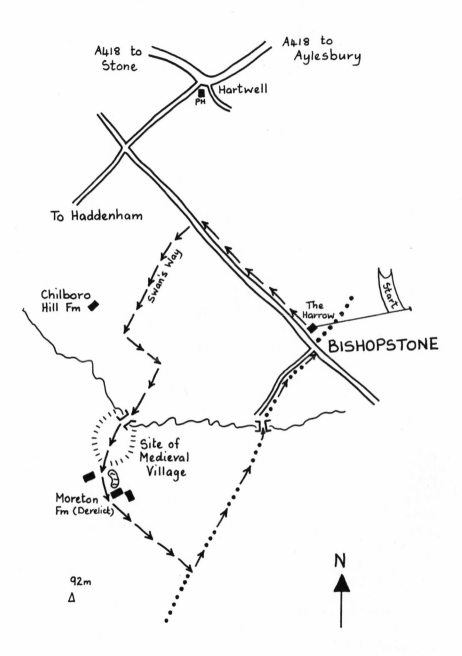

A418 to Stone

A418 to Aylesbury

Hartwell

PH

To Haddenham

Swan's Way

Chilboro Hill Fm

The Harrow

Start

BISHOPSTONE

Site of Medieval Village

Moreton Fm (Derelict)

92m
Δ

N

above sea level. Down to the bottom corner of this field the route leaves the Swan's Way as it turns left and follows the combined North Bucks Way/Midshires Way along the line of the hedge.

The headland path passes two large, white willow trees and continues along the hedge which, during the summer months, is alive with the orangey-brown fluttering of gate-keeper butterflies. The route continues through a five-bar gate and follows the hedge across a pasture before crossing a bridge over a small stream followed by a stile next to a metal gate. From here the track becomes Moreton Lane, which runs past cottages and then a large farm on the outskirts of Bishopstone. The lane meets a road at a T-junction opposite the war memorial. Here, the pub walk turns left and follows the road past the waymarked track on the right for the North Bucks/Midshires Way.

A hundred yards or so along the road you reach the Harrow on the right.

Midshires Way – Bishopstone to Hartwell (1½ miles)

A short stretch which leaves to the right of the Harrow (see above). The route follows the North Bucks Way on a track across mainly arable fields. At a cross-tracks it turns left, along a hedged track which, eventually, runs through the picturesque hamlet of Sedrup. From here, the track becomes a narrow lane which continues past Galley Farmhouse before arriving on the outskirts of Hartwell to the rear of the Bugle Horn, on the A418. From this pub, which lies directly on the route of the Midshires Way, the route is described in Pub Walk 3.

[3] Hartwell
The Bugle Horn

Upper and Lower Hartwell lie mainly off the busy A418 to nearby Aylesbury. The village is best known for Hartwell House, a Jacobean mansion sympathetically restored to its former glories by Historic House Hotels.

Previously a coaching inn, the Bugle Horn is a large, rambling building set back from the main road. Inside, spacious accommodation is provided by an open-plan L-shaped bar with a separate, comfortable snug at one end and a very pleasant conservatory at the other. Wood panelling decorated with hunting prints together with a combination of settles, chairs and tables creates a comfortable, 'country' atmosphere. The servery provides inviting home-cooked meals complemented by an extensive range of fresh salads. Long-established favourites such as steak and kidney pie compete with an array of dishes such as quiche, pastrami and Cumberland sausage. During the summer months a barbecue in the award winning garden provides a good choice of charcoal-grilled fish and meat, including lamb Mehsen, specially prepared and cooked by the landlord to a secret recipe! The large garden and patio area to the rear of the pub includes a well-equipped children's play area.

The Bugle Horn is an Ind Coope (Benskins) pub serving Tetley Bitter,

Wadworth 6X, and Burton Ale. An additional guest beer is changed regularly throughout the year. Guinness, two lagers and cider are also available on draught.

The opening times are Monday to Friday from 11.30 am to 3 pm, and 6 pm to 11 pm. On Saturdays and Sundays the pub opens all day. Telephone: 01296 748209.

How to get there: Hartwell is only 2 miles south-west of Aylesbury on the A418. The pub is on the main road, almost opposite the entrance to Hartwell House.

Parking: There are two large car parks to one side of the pub.

Length of the walk: 4¹/₂ miles (shorter option possible). Map: OS Landranger 165 Aylesbury and Leighton Buzzard (inn GR 795121).

An interesting walk across very attractive countryside to Eythrope Park in the Thame Valley and back. Apart from nearby Hartwell House, this is mainly Rothschild country, part of the fiefdom of this fabulously wealthy and powerful banking family which left its mark on the surrounding villages and countryside in so many ways.

The walk also includes a chance to see Buckinghamshire's only 'Egyptian' well, plus a mysterious new statue on the banks of the river Thame.

The Walk

From the pub the route turns left, along the main road which is crossed to follow a lane on the right signposted to nearby Hartwell House.

This impressive mansion, once the court in exile of King Louis XVIII of France, is now an exclusive hotel patronised by the rich and famous – most recently President Clinton made a radio broadcast to America from the library. Those curious for a closer look can obtain the key to the church within its grounds from the hotel's reception desk.

The route stays with the lane up and past Woodbine Cottage then down a small hill, at the bottom of which stands an 'Egyptian' well, complete with hieroglyphics. Once, it also bore an inscription in Greek stating 'water is best'! Past here the route leaves the lane as it turns left, over a stile waymarked for the North Bucks Way.

Across stiles each side of two pastures it meets a lane to the right of a thatched cottage on the outskirts of Upper Hartwell. Here it turns right for a few yards, then left over a stile next to a gate. A short stretch of concrete track leads to another stile over which the hedge is followed to a waymarked oak post where the path angles right, across the pasture

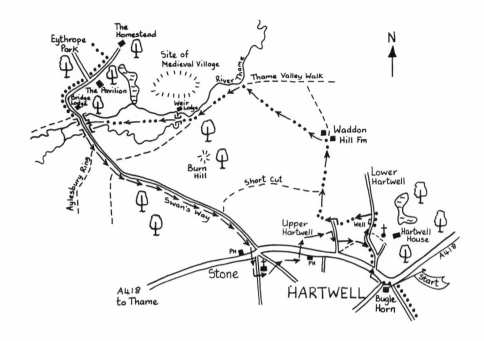

to a footbridge and stile. A headland path follows the hedge uphill and eventually past the buildings of Waddon Hill Farm. At a T-junction a track is followed left, across the front of three large barns, beyond which it eventually runs downhill to a gap in the hedge. From here a path bears diagonally right, across an arable field, and then continues along the hedge. Through another metal stile it keeps ahead and is joined by the Thame Valley Walk down to the banks of the river Thame. Here it turns left and, after a short distance, where the river bends right, the route bears away from the river through a swing-gate. After following a headland path round an arable field, it turns right, through two five-bar gates, back to the river. Having turned left along the river bank, the path continues to a footbridge and weir where Weir Lodge on the opposite bank makes as pretty a river-side scene as any likely to be found in the county. North of here once stood the medieval village of Eythrope from which the park gets its name.

Over the weir a path leads to a concrete farm road which is followed across wide pastures. On the other side a track continues through mature trees bordering the river. Through the trees to the right there are occasional glimpses of the lake next to the Pavilion, originally built as a grandiose country retreat for Nancy de Rothschild. Further along on the left awaits the second surprise of this walk in the shape of a stone

25

bust, standing close to the river in the shelter of the trees. The statue is obviously fairly new and the absence of any inscription adds to its air of mystery – is it, perhaps, a likeness of Nancy who so loved this place? At the end of the track the pub walk turns left and leaves the route of the North Bucks/Midshires Way, which turns right, heading north across Eythrope Park.

The pub walk stays with the estate road as it climbs up out of the Thame Valley. After the road flattens out, the route passes through a gate, beyond which a path on the left provides a convenient short-cut (see map). The main walk, however, keeps ahead down to and across the main road to follow a narrow lane opposite. Within 100 yards a footpath on the left takes it through a churchyard, up to and past St John the Baptist church and down to another lane. Across this, the path continues via swing-gates either side of a small pasture to a recreation field, across which the route turns left, back over the main road. A track or drive opposite leads to a thatched cottage in front of which it turns right, on a path which runs along the bottom of gardens. At a lane it turns right for about 50 yards before turning left, on a fenced path across fields. Bearing left at a Y-junction the path follows a boundary wall to meet another lane to the right of Woodbine Cottage, passed earlier. Here, it turns right, and the route is retraced, back to the Bugle Horn.

Midshires Way – Hartwell to Waddesdon (5 miles)

From Hartwell, the route is described in detail as far as the estate road in Eythrope Park (see above). The route stays with the North Bucks Way which turns right, across the bridge and along to Bridge Lodge. Here it turns right again, through a gate and follows the estate road ahead. After bending right it keeps ahead over a crossroads before turning off left, just before the gates to the Homestead, on the Swan's Way bridletrack. At a T-junction it turns right and follows an uphill track which leaves Eythrope Park at North Lodge. From here the route is described in detail as part of Pub Walk 4, from the Five Arrows, Waddesdon.

[4]　Waddesdon
The Five Arrows Hotel

The village is well known because of its proximity to Waddesdon Manor, built in the 1870s for Baron Ferdinand de Rothschild. Many of the buildings in the village, including the hotel, were built by the Rothschilds and bear the family crest of a crown and five arrows.

The ornate, Victorian style of the Five Arrows Hotel is pleasingly complemented by hanging baskets of geraniums and lobelias, whilst the interior has recently been completely and sympathetically refurbished. Hotel accommodation is at a premium during the summer months when booking in advance is advisable. Informality with style creates a friendly and welcoming atmosphere in the two main rooms. These are served by a long, L-shaped bar at the end of which there are two additional and very comfortable rooms. Victorian photographs portray life in old Waddesdon whilst the Rothschild connection extends to a selection of wines from the famous vineyards that bear the family name. The hotel's award winning Mediterranean-style cuisine includes such dishes as French onion tart with mixed leaf salad or Greek-style lamb with oregano. Reasonably priced bar meals include a good choice of sandwiches with a variety of generous fillings, traditional ploughman's and beefy American burgers. A vegetarian choice is always available whilst a barbecue in the garden provides al fresco meals on Saturdays throughout the summer.

The Five Arrows Hotel is a freehouse and serves locally brewed cask conditioned beers, such as Old Icknield from the Tring Brewery, and Beechwood Bitter from the Chiltern Brewery. Fuller's London Pride plus a guest beer that changes regularly completes an interesting choice of real ales. Draught lager is also available. In addition, the hotel takes pride in its wine list and the choice of over 30 malt whiskies.

During the summer the opening times are Monday to Saturday from 11 am to 11 pm; during the winter, from 11 am to 3 pm and 6 pm to 11 pm. Sunday, from noon to 3 pm and 7 pm to 10.30 pm.

Telephone: 01296 651727.

How to get there: Waddesdon is 5 miles north-west of Aylesbury on the A41(T) to Bicester. The hotel is on the main road at the western end of the village.

Parking: There is a car park in the courtyard behind the hotel.

Length of the walk: 4 miles (shorter option possible). Map: OS Landranger 165 Aylesbury and Leighton Buzzard (inn GR 742168).

A walk through open parkland surrounding Waddesdon Manor, one of the five great houses built in the Vale of Aylesbury by the Rothschilds in the second half of the 19th century.

The Walk
From the hotel the route turns left, along to the war memorial. Here, it turns left again and follows the narrow estate road used as the exit route from nearby Waddesdon Manor. The main entrance to Waddesdon Manor is a few hundred yards further along the main road. Waddesdon Manor is open to the public from March to October. Once the home of the Rothschilds, it was bequeathed to the nation by James de Rothschild and is now a National Trust property. An impressive French-style chateau set in formal, Victorian parkland, it contains important collections of art and furniture. Telephone: 01296 651282. The walk continues past Princes Lodge and through the gates into Waddesdon estate. Past the Bowling Club on the right, it continues ahead along a short stretch of road which is open to walkers with the permission of the estate. At a T-junction it turns left, then right, down a gated estate road which traverses open parkland as it heads south. This part of the walk provides easy, pleasant walking with the chance to spot deer grazing between wooded areas that provide cover for birds and other wildlife. The road bears left across the bottom of the shallow

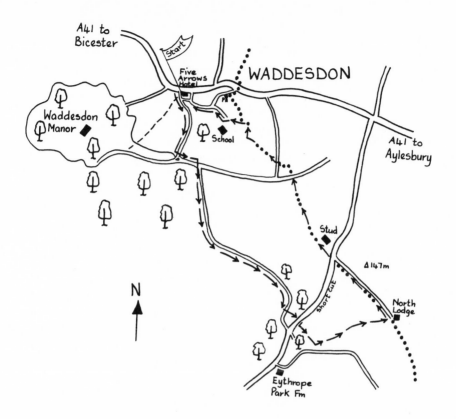

valley, then turns right as it climbs back up through a wooded area of mainly broad-leaved trees. Before the road bends left again, the route leaves the estate road as it turns left, to pass in front of a large fir tree. From here a path runs through mature trees followed by a new plantation up to the road.

At this point a short-cut can be taken by turning left, along the grass verge, and following the road down to the stables belonging to Waddesdon Stud (see sketch map). The main route, however, crosses the road diagonally to the right and goes over a stile from which a path follows a wooden railed fence to the left of a wood. Just round the corner of the field it turns right, and runs downhill through more trees to emerge via a swing-gate to the left of another estate road. Here, it turns left to follow a headland track along the edge of wide, arable fields across which there are good views south, over Aylesbury Vale. Eventually, the track reaches a T-junction behind North Lodge, where it turns left, along the North Bucks/Midshires Way.

29

Past the lodge the track becomes a narrow lane which runs over Waddesdon Hill and down to the road crossed earlier. Here, the route crosses straight over and continues ahead on a metalled drive past the immaculate stables complex of Waddesdon Stud. Where the driveway ends, a path keeps ahead through a narrow wood to stiles each side of a paddock from which there are good views of distant Waddesdon Manor. The path bears left, down through a plantation of saplings, to another stile over which it continues downhill, following the line of a recently planted hedge. At the bottom of the valley it crosses stiles each side of another estate road. From here it clips the corner of an arable field as it angles left, then follows a fence and path leading past the end of a large barn to a roadside stile. The road is crossed diagonally right, to pick up a path which runs across a stream and through a belt of trees to another stile. From here the path crosses an arable field, on the other side of which it turns right, along a fenced path running round the perimeter of school playing fields. After turning left, it runs past the gardens of houses on the outskirts of Waddesdon. The pub walk then continues ahead past a waymarked stile on the right, where the North Bucks/Midshires Way turns off, and heads north.

After another left turn, the (now) tarmac path arrives at the main gates to the school, where the route turns right, down School Lane. At the T-junction it turns left, along Baker Street, and continues ahead on a fenced path where the road bends to the right. Where the path meets the road walked earlier, the route is retraced back to the Five Arrows Hotel.

Midshires Way – Waddesdon to Quainton (2 miles)

From Eythrope Park's North Lodge, the route is described in detail as far as the school on the outskirts of Waddesdon (see above). From here the route turns right along the North Bucks Way across allotments. At the road it turns right, down to and across the A41. Clear of the houses, it continues ahead over several pastures before keeping to the right of farm buildings and a pond. It then turns left, over a fence, and right, along a concrete track which it leaves as it keeps ahead down a long pasture and over a railway line. Aiming for Quainton windmill, more pastures are crossed before arriving on the forecourt of the White Hart. The route turns left, along the road to the village green and right, up past the George and Dragon. From here it is described in Pub Walk 5.

[5] Quainton
The George and Dragon

Dominated by Quainton Hill, which looms behind it, this attractive village has a green at its centre which in turn is dominated by the restored tower windmill at its top end. Picturesque cottages and houses face onto and cluster round the green, on the right-hand side of which stands the George and Dragon, a typical village pub.

Inside, there are two separate bars, a public bar with the usual accoutrements and, down a wide stone step on the right, a comfortably furnished lounge bar. Low, wooden beams and red-brick arches create a snug and cosy refuge in which to enjoy a wide choice of home-cooked pub grub. The pies, such as steak and Stilton, or beef cooked in Guinness, are very popular, as is the traditional fish and chips. Less traditional but equally delicious are the oriental king prawns and paella. There is always a choice of several vegetarian dishes and children are catered for. Several picnic style tables are sited in front of the pub, facing the village green. Meals are not served on Mondays or on Sunday evenings.

The George and Dragon serves three cask conditioned bitters, Tetley Bitter, Webster's Yorkshire Bitter, and Benskins Best Bitter. Beamish, Guinness, two lagers and a cider are also available on draught. Wines are

31

available by the bottle or glass, plus a wine of the month by the jug.
The opening hours are Monday to Saturday from 12 noon to 2.30 pm
and 6 pm to 11 pm, and on Sunday from 12 noon to 3 pm and 7 pm to
10.30 pm.
Telephone: 01296 655436.

How to get there: Quainton is about 5 miles north-west of Aylesbury.
Turn off the A413 (Aylesbury to Buckingham) at Whitchurch, or the
A41 (Aylesbury to Bicester) at Waddesdon, to follow minor roads. The
pub is on the village green.

Parking: There is a parking area to one side of the pub plus roadside
parking around the village green.

Length of the walk: 4 miles, with shorter option. Map: OS Landranger
165 Aylesbury and Leighton Buzzard (inn GR 746202).

*A walk from a picturesque village with much to see, up and
over Quainton Hill, 187 metres above sea-level. Panoramic views
across Aylesbury Vale to the Chilterns on one side and as far as
the distant Cotswolds on the other make this a truly memorable
walk.*

The Walk

From the pub the route turns right, up the side of the village
green. At the top it turns left, along the road running across the
top of the green, just below the restored windmill. This windmill, the
tallest in the county, is open to visitors on Sunday mornings, and
would make an interesting start, or ending, to the walk. Just past the
windmill an information board on the right gives historical information
concerning the windmill and other notable buildings plus details of the
nearby Buckinghamshire Railway Centre. Telephone: 01296 655450.

Across the top of the green also runs an old stone path or causeway
to the remains of the preaching cross which is thought to pre-date the
village church. Where the green ends, the route continues ahead along
Upper Street. Opposite a small playing field it turns right, between two
white houses, on a track waymarked for the North Bucks Way. The
track soon becomes a stony path which runs up to a swing-gate on the
lower slopes of Quainton Hill. From here, a grassy path climbs ahead
aiming to the left of the TV mast seen on the summit. There is an
excellent view of the nearby windmill up to the first stile, and, as the path
continues to climb, the views across Aylesbury Vale and the surrounding
countryside could only be bettered from a not-so-low-flying aircraft!

Eventually, after briefly dipping down, the grassy track reaches an

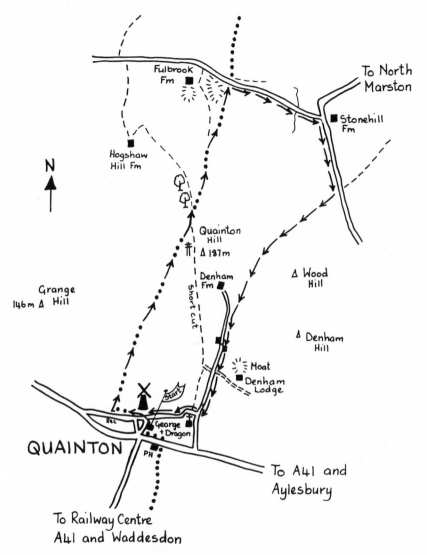

area where the bumps and hollows of old stone workings provide a convenient place to enjoy wonderful views stretching from the Chilterns in the south, to the distant Cotswolds in the north-west. Over another stile the route bears right across a pasture and follows the hedge along to a swing-gate and stile on the right. The path again follows the hedge up to a gate on top of the ridge to the rear of the nearby TV mast. (From here the short-cut turns right, through the gate, and follows the track back down to a farm road leading into the village.)

The main route, however, stays with the Midshires Way as it turns left, along the line of the ridge, and crosses to another swing-gate. Wide views to the north and east open up as the route now bears to the right, down the flank of the hill. There is no distinct path, but a line is taken to the left of the mound below, aiming for a wooden footbridge at the base of the hill, to the right of a farm gate. From here it keeps ahead across two more pastures where this time bumps and hollows mark the site of an abandoned medieval village, next to which now stands Fulbrook Farm. Over the roadside stile the route leaves the Midshires/North Bucks Way, which continues ahead.

The pub walk turns right, along the narrow, gated road which, after crossing a stream, turns right at a T-junction and runs up a small hill. At the top of the hill it flattens out and, after a short distance, the route leaves the road again as it turns right, over a stile next to a fingerpost. From here the path crosses a pasture at the bottom of the hill; climb this aiming to the left of the TV mast seen earlier in the walk. Over the hilltop it runs down between a large tree and a smaller stump, behind which a stile in a wooden railed fence takes the path diagonally right, across another pasture. From a last stile in the hedge, it continues down the south face of the hill, with Denham Farm down in the hollow to the right. Again, there are wide views to the south as the path runs down to the farm access road along which the route turns left. Past houses each side of a cattle-grid, Denham Lodge can be seen across the pasture on the left.

The road continues ahead across a junction where the short-cut track from the TV mast comes in from the right. Over another cattle grid it becomes a metalled lane which runs past a row of estate cottages on the outskirts of Quainton. At the T-junction it turns right, along Church Street and past the village church which stands next to a row of attractive almshouses. A short distance further on is the village stores which sells a modestly priced guide to the history of the village. At the village green the route turns left, back down to the George and Dragon.

Midshires Way – Quainton to Verney Junction (5 miles)

From the village green the route is described in detail as far as the lane on the other side of Quainton Hill (see above). The route continues with the North Bucks Way across relatively flat farmland to a road, along which it turns left. Opposite the entrance to Lower Farm, a path on the right takes the route into East Claydon. At the centre of the village, it forks right and leaves Sandhill Road on a path to the right which crosses undulating farmland to another road, just outside Verney Junction. From here the route is described in Pub Walk 6 from the Bell, Winslow.

[6] Winslow
The Bell Hotel

Winslow is a small market town centred around a square lined with attractive buildings: one of these is the Bell Hotel. The handsome, columnar door and the bay windows of the Bell Hotel overlook the southern end of the square, where an inn has stood since Tudor times. Today, it offers elegant yet homely accommodation, whilst the evident good nature and helpfulness of the couple who own and manage this one-time coaching inn ensures a warm welcome. Heavy oak beams and open, ingle-nook fireplaces, antique furniture and luxurious carpeting all make this the epitome of a comfortable, English country inn. Apart from the two main bars, there is a coffee lounge and a split-level dining-room. There is a wide range of traditional home-cooked bar meals, such as steak and kidney pudding, or sandwiches of Desperate Dan proportions – much appreciated by hungry farmers on market days. The carvery menu, midday Sundays and evenings throughout the week, specialises in succulent roasts, including roast sirloin of Buckinghamshire beef with Yorkshire pudding, or roast turkey with all the trimmings. A vegetarian choice is always available.

The Bell Hotel is a freehouse and serves Greene King Abbot Ale and IPA from the cask. Guinness, two lagers and cider are also available on draught.

As a hotel, the Bell is open Monday to Saturday from 10 am to 10.30 pm. On Sundays the usual licensing hours apply, from 12 noon to 3 pm and 7 pm to 10.30 pm.

A courtyard to the rear provides a very pleasant area in which to enjoy a warm summer's evening. Dogs are welcome in the courtyard.

Telephone: 01296 712741/714091.

How to get there: Winslow is on the A413, 5 miles south-east of Buckingham. The Bell is at the centre of the town, on the main road at the southern end of the market square.

Parking: There is a large car park to one side and to the rear of the inn.

Length of the walk: 4½ miles (shorter option possible). Map: OS Landranger 165 Aylesbury and Leighton Buzzard (inn GR 770275).

A walk over typical mid-Buckinghamshire farmland to Verney Junction, once an important station on the old Metropolitan line. From here it returns via the isolated and very private hamlet of Addington, with good views across the countryside to the south.

The Walk
From the Bell the route runs up the High Street, past the end of the market square, and turns left, along an alley which runs to the parish church of St Laurence. The church is well worth a visit for its 15th century wall paintings. (A short distance down Market Street the house and gardens of Winslow Hall are open to the public on Wednesday and Thursday afternoons during July and August. Telephone: 01296 712323.) Past the church, the path bends left, down between some picturesque houses and turns right, along Horn Street. Where the road bends left, the route crosses straight over and continues along Western Lane. As this road bends right, it keeps ahead, over a stile, then along a fenced path behind new houses.

Another stile takes the path across rough pasture, after which it keeps to the left of stables and round a large heap of mucked-out straw and down to a stile, where it turns right. Over a pasture it passes through a swing-gate followed by a five-bar gate. From here the path follows the hedge to a stile, after which it crosses a field, keeping to the left of a pylon to another stile. After two more fields and footbridges, the hedge is followed to a metal gate. Here the route turns right, under the old railway arch, on the other side of which it turns left, along the bottom of the railway embankment. In the corner of this last field, a stile leads to the road, along which the route turns left.

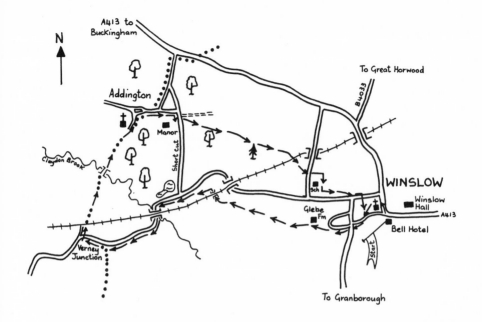

A short distance along the road a turning off to the right is signposted to Addington. Take this uphill lane for the short-cut. Look for the Cross Bucks Way footpath on the right at the top of the hill next to a white gate. The main route, however, continues ahead and, after passing under the railway line again, stays with the road past where the North Bucks/Midshires Way comes in on the left.

Further along the road, opposite the Verney Arms at Verney Junction, the route turns right, on a no-through road. Within a short distance the old station master's house is passed and the route bears right, across the railway line. Through a swing-gate, it follows the hedge before crossing a stile and track, then a footbridge at the top end of the field. Across a pasture and a substantial footbridge over Claydon Brook, the path runs over an arable field, to the right of the church tower ahead. Across a second stile and a short field it arrives at a lane along which it turns left. Past the church, it bears right at a Y-junction.

A short detour down the lane to the left is an impressive farm complex which includes the oldest cruciform barn in the county, in front of which the old village stocks have been built into the wall.

Further on the route continues ahead past the main entrance to Addington Manor, opposite which the North Bucks/Midshires Way leaves as it follows the road left.

The pub walk continues ahead to a T-junction, where it turns right, then leaves the lane as it turns left over a stile next to a white gate. From here the route joins the Cross Bucks Way which runs diagonally right, along the ridge-top pasture from which there are wide views across the countryside to the south.

Clipping the corner of a small wood, it continues in the same direction down to stile in the bottom corner of the field. From here the path bears right across an arable field to a footbridge and stile in the far corner. Over another stile at the corner of the wood on the right, the path continues to head roughly in the same direction as it slopes down over two more pastures and a stream to the railway line, which is crossed for the last time. Over the railway line a series of stiles and footbridges take the path to a lane which the route crosses straight over. The path now follows a chain-link fence round the perimeter of a school, before going through a swing-gate, after which the path bears left, over rough pasture behind houses. Over a last stile on the right, a fenced path leads to the road along which the route turns left. Past Parsons Close, it turns right, on a cycle path leading down to Horn Street. Here, the route turns left, back to the Bell.

Midshires Way – Verney Junction to Whaddon (7 miles)

From Verney Junction the route is described in detail as far as Addington (see above). The route stays with the North Bucks Way which turns left, along a lane up to the A413. Here it turns right, before leaving the road on a track to the left across fields to Great Horwood (B&B available at Grange Stables, telephone: 01296 712051). After passing through the village it turns left, off the road, and crosses the A421 and arable farmland before skirting the village of Nash. From here, a track becomes a headland path leading to Whaddon, beyond which the route is described in Pub Walk 7, from the Lowndes Arms (B&B available, telephone: 01908 501706).

[7] Whaddon
The Lowndes Arms

Whaddon is situated on high ground in the centre of what was Whaddon Chase, once the hunting preserves of royalty. Today, the great forest has gone, but the village survives as a very pleasant and still rural place, now virtually on the fringes of the rapidly expanding new town of Milton Keynes.

The Lowndes Arms is named after the family that once lived in nearby Whaddon Hall. Originally, as a hostelry in hunting country, it was more appropriately known as 'The Haunch of Venison'. Built as a coaching inn complete with stables and forge, it still offers eleven bedrooms and a separate function room on the site of the old stables. The forge has been incorporated into the spacious main building. A huge ingle-nook fireplace dominates one end of the open plan bar to the front, whilst to the rear is a very pleasant dining-room. Separate tables with high-backed wooden chairs and stools provide a flexible combination over which a collection of highly burnished brasses hang from exposed oak beams.

Renowned for its rump steaks, the inn provides home cooking which ranges from appetisers, such as lobster bisque, or smoked salmon and prawn platter, to an ever expanding choice of 'specials' such as the popular tiger prawns wrapped in bacon with garlic and sliced mushrooms. All the sweets are home-made and there is always a selection of vegetarian dishes. Meals are available seven days a week. A garden to the rear provides a very pleasant spot from which to enjoy the views across open countryside.

The Lowndes Arms keeps a good choice of real ales, including Ruddles County, Draught Bass, Courage Directors, Tetley Bitter, ABC Best Bitter, and Benskins Best Bitter. Guinness, three lagers and two ciders are also available on draught.

The opening times are Monday to Saturday from 11 am to 3 pm and 6 pm to 11 pm, and on Sunday from 12 noon to 10.30 pm.

Telephone: 01908 501706.

How to get there: Whaddon is on the south-west side of Milton Keynes, just 3 miles from the town centre. Turn off the A5 onto the A421 or the A422 to Buckingham. The village lies between the two roads, with the inn at its centre.

Parking: There is a car park to the rear of the inn.

Length of the walk: 3¹/₂ miles. Map: OS Landranger 152 Northampton and Milton Keynes (inn GR 806343).

A walk through a still rural landscape on the fringes of the new town. Here the past is still much in evidence, from the village church, parts of which date back beyond the 14th century, to the site of Snelshall Priory, founded in 1219.

The Walk

From the inn the route turns left, along the road up to the T-junction which it crosses straight over to follow a narrow drive signposted to the church. Where the drive ends, a footpath continues ahead through the churchyard, going round the left-hand side of the church.

St Mary's church stands four square to the winds on its exposed site and inside has much of interest, including brass effigies on the tomb of Sergeant Pigott (died 1519) and an early weight-driven clock of 1673.

Behind the church the route joins the North Bucks/Midshires Way which follows Church Lane down to the road. Here, it turns right, staying with the road past Vicarage Road and Oak Tree Cottage with its Punch and Judy like figures dated 1865. The main road turns right, but the route continues ahead along a lane for a few yards before turning left, down Briary View. Past the end of the new houses, a swing-gate marks the continuation of the North Bucks/Midshires Way on a headland track following the hedge across a wide field. Another swing-gate takes the path to a second wide field and keeps ahead along

40

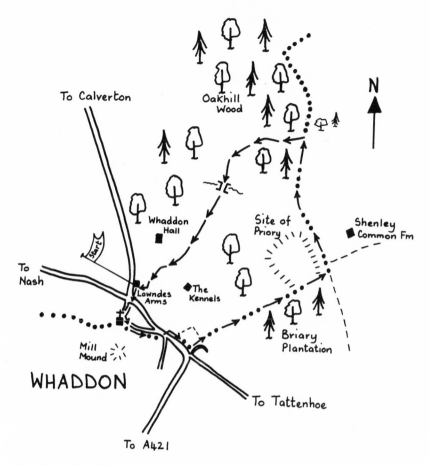

To Calverton

Oakhill
Wood

N

To
Nash

Whaddon
Hall

Site of
Priory

Shenley
Common Fm

Lowndes
Arms

The
Kennels

Mill
Mound

WHADDON

Briary
Plantation

To Tattenhoe

To A421

the line of a ditch on the other side of which is Briary Plantation.
Towards the top corner of this field wide ditches mark the boundary
lines of Snelshall Priory, a Benedictine monastery founded in the early
13th century. Several ancient oaks give the appearance of having been
here almost as long but, of the ancient buildings, nothing now remains.

Through another swing-gate in the top corner of the field, the route
turns left, along a hedged track and through two more gates each end
of a narrow pasture. The path now keeps ahead up rising ground on a
path to the right of Oakhill Wood. Opposite where a new plantation of
trees begins on the right, the pub walk turns left, and leaves the North
Bucks/Midshires Way, which continues ahead.

Via a gate on the left, the walk follows a designated Countryside Route
through dense woodland, alive with the rustle of hidden wildlife. At the

41

wood's edge a stile is crossed and the path runs diagonally left, down to the bottom corner of an arable field. Over another stile the path turns left and follows the hedge to a second stile which takes it across a stream and over a track. From here the route crosses diagonally right over a wide field, aiming for a stile on the far side on the lower slopes of the hill. Across this, the path runs uphill, keeping to the left of the pond, and over the top of the hill. From here there are good views across the countryside recently traversed and a close-up of Whaddon Hall, built in 1820, on the site of a much earlier mansion.

From this stile the path crosses a pasture, aiming for the church tower passed earlier. A five-bar gate takes it along a fenced track and a final stile on the right takes the walk through the car park behind the Lowndes Arms.

Midshires Way – Whaddon to Loughton (3½ miles)

From Whaddon the route is described in detail as far as Oakhill Wood (see above). The route continues ahead to a junction at the top of the rise, now in company with the Swan's Way, which is followed through Milton Keynes and beyond, to Salcey Forest on the Northamptonshire border. Having turned right, a track is followed ahead to the left of Shenley Wood for about ½ mile to the first main road. Here, it turns right, then left, under the road on a Redway, part of a network of paths throughout Milton Keynes. From here Midshires Way/Swan's Way waymarks are followed via paths and lanes down to a T-junction to the right of the church at Shenley Church End. Here the route turns right and, at a second roundabout, it goes through Loughton Underpass and continues ahead. From here the route is described in Pub Walk 8, from the Fountain, Loughton (Milton Keynes).

B&B is available at the Corner House, Loughton, telephone: 01908 605321.

[8] Loughton
The Fountain

Loughton is one of the ancient villages now incorporated into Milton Keynes itself. The Fountain survives from a time when it was an important staging post on old Watling Street and the discovery of this long, thatched building, on the fringes of a modern town, comes as a welcome surprise. Recently incorporated into the Harvester chain, run by Forte, the original timbers and flagstones at the heart of the building form the basis for a rustic theme. Low ceilings, large open fireplaces and exposed brickwork complement furniture, fixtures and fittings designed to enhance the rural appearance of its interior. A long bar serves comfortable, open plan areas off which recesses provide separate seating. At the far end a recent extension built from re-cycled timbers is designed to heighten the 'olde worlde' atmosphere, whilst kitchen business can be observed off-stage through the open serving hatches.

In addition to a good selection of value for money bar meals, the busy restaurant is popular for its char-grilled steaks and fish. Specialities are Smokes and Marinades such as spit roast chicken and slow roast lamb. Another feature is a salad cart from which a wide range of ingredients and dressings allows for the creation of individual salads. Vegetarians and children are catered for and meals are available seven days a week. There is a large garden to the rear of the pub complete with purpose built barbecue for the summer months. Dogs are welcome in the garden.

Cask ales on offer include Courage Directors, Courage Best Bitter and Ruddles County. John Smith's Bitter, two lagers and cider are also available on draught.

The opening hours are Monday to Friday from 11 am to 3 pm, and 5 pm to 11 pm and on Saturday from 11 am to 11 pm. Sunday from 12 noon to 3 pm and 7 pm to 10.30 pm.

Telephone: 01908 666203.

How to get there: Loughton is now a south-western district of Milton Keynes between Stony Stratford and Bletchley, off the A5, just 1 mile from the town centre. The pub can most easily be reached by turning off Watling Street between Childs Way and Portway.

Parking: There is limited parking in front of the inn, with ample parking to the rear.

Length of the walk: 2½ miles (shorter and longer options possible). Map: OS Landranger 152 Northampton and Milton Keynes (inn GR 836371).

A walk to Lodge Lake in Loughton Valley Park, part of a wide network of recreation and outdoor leisure facilities throughout the town. Wildlife, including water-fowl, thrives and occasional herons compete with anglers on lakes well-stocked with fish. The walk returns via the ancient village of Loughton, where rural tranquillity still survives in the heart of this new town.

The Walk

From the Fountain the route turns left, on the roadside path. Past Hillcrest Close, where the road ends, a path on the left leads down to join the Swan's Way/Midshires Way in front of an underpass.

The route turns left along a Redway footpath with the Swan's Way bridletrack on the other side of the wooden fence. The path forks left, between houses and across two service roads, before crossing a third road to an artificial mound created as a viewing platform across the city. Ahead can be seen Loughton church and village. To the right the prominent dome of the new church stands out at the town centre, which also boasts one of the largest indoor shopping centres in Europe and The Point, a futuristic, pyramidal shaped cinema and leisure complex.

Over the mound another road is crossed and the route turns left, then right, down Whitworth Lane. Where the lane bends left, a view board on

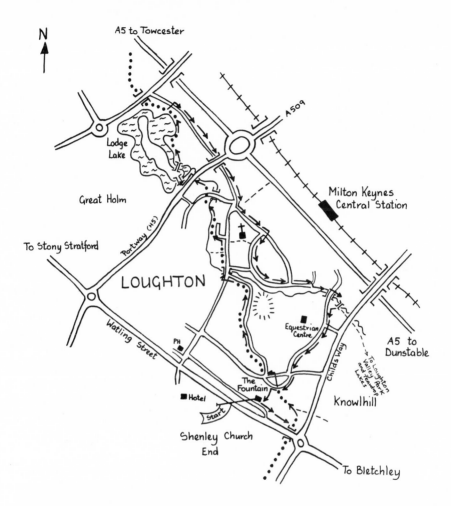

the right gives details of local history. At the T-junction, the route turns right, to follow the road over a bridge and past a thatched house on the outskirts of Loughton village. It then continues ahead, past a footpath on the right which can be taken as a short-cut and which runs up to the village church.

Past here the route turns left, down Lucy Lane and, where the lane turns right, it continues ahead on a waymarked path and track. The Swan's Way bridletrack fords a small stream, but stepping stones or a road bridge to the right can be used by walkers. Over the stream, the route crosses the road to the left of the bridge and continues along the valley running under a main road (H5). It then bends left before meeting

45

the first lake, where it turns right over a red bridge. The path and the bridletrack follow the banks of the lake at the top of which the route turns right, over another bridge and then left, along to Lodge Lake. At the top of this lake the route leaves the Swan's Way/Midshires Way as it turns off right, at a fingerpost in front of a small car park.

From here the path runs to a nearby road along which the route turns right, on a roadside path. After passing the National Badminton Centre on the left, and Herons Lodge on the right, it passes back under the main road. Crossing to the other side of the road, the path continues up a rise. At the top a fingerpost is passed before the route turns left, along a narrow lane leading to the centre of the old village. At a T-junction in front of All Saints Church, parts of which date back to the 13th century, it turns right, and runs downhill. Past the old school complete with bell, it carries on down to a junction at the bottom of the hill. Here, it turns left, in front of the Wheatsheaf village stores, once the village pub. Past cottages and a lane coming in from the left, the lane continues ahead before bending left. Here, the route bears right, on a path with a sign for Loughton Valley Park and Teardrop Lakes. The path follows a stream up to and straight over a road, after which the route turns right, across a wooden footbridge over the stream. At a small, roadside car park, a view board gives details relating to the park and the lakes. A network of paths throughout the park could be used either as an extension to this pub walk, or serve as an excellent basis for future walking and exploration.

Through the car park, the route rejoins and turns left along the road which runs up past Loughton Manor Equestrian Centre to a crossroads at the top of the rise. Here the route crosses straight over and keeps to the left of the mound crossed earlier. Across the path walked earlier and past the mound, it turns left, to follow a metalled path in front of a large ash tree. From here, the path runs up to the road, where the route turns right, back down to the Fountain.

Midshires Way – Loughton to New Bradwell (3 miles)

From Loughton the route is described in detail as far as Lodge Lake (see above). Still with the Swan's Way, it first crosses a main road and continues north. Under the A5, it passes the site of Bradwell Abbey, which is within walking distance of the city's Youth Hostel (telephone: 01908 310944). Under the railway line, it turns left, just before a stream, and under the A422, beyond which it reaches the famous concrete cows. From here the route is described in Pub Walk 9, from the New Inn, New Bradwell.

[9] New Bradwell
The New Inn

New Bradwell is another old village now incorporated into Milton Keynes. The New Inn stands on the banks of the Grand Union canal, a good, honest, unpretentious pub run very much as a family affair. Accommodation is spacious with a separate lounge and public bar, plus a pool room. The bars are comfortably furnished and, in the lounge, brass gleams and the walls display a collection of old canal photographs. Upstairs, there is a surprisingly large and very pleasant restaurant where Saturday night dinner dances are a speciality. Very reasonably priced bar meals include popular home-made steak and kidney pies, whilst the restaurant is well known for chef's specials such as beef Wellington. There is a children's menu and meals are available seven days a week. Behind the pub is a patio and small garden complete with an aviary presided over by Sadie the goat. In addition, there is a grassed area to the front which overlooks the canal. Well-behaved dogs are allowed in the bars if kept on a lead.

The New Inn is a Charles Wells pub and serves their Eagle IPA, Bombardier Best Bitter, plus the recently re-introduced Wells Fargo, in addition to Adnams Broadside, Morland Old Speckled Hen and 'specials', such as Theakston XB and Charles Wells Noggin. Guinness, three lagers and cider are also available on draught.

The opening times are Monday to Saturday from 11 am to 11 pm, and on Sunday from 12 noon to 3 pm and 7 pm to 10.30 pm.

Telephone: 01908 312094.

How to get there: New Bradwell is in the northern district of Milton Keynes between Stony Stratford and Newport Pagnell. Turn off the A422 between the A5 and the M1. The pub is on the southern side of the Grand Union canal, near Bradwell Windmill.

Parking: There is ample car parking on two sides of the inn.

Length of the walk: 3½ miles (shorter option possible). Map: OS Landranger 152 Northampton and Milton Keynes (inn GR 832413).

A walk that includes close encounters of a concrete kind with the famous Milton Keynes cows. A modern aqueduct on the Grand Union canal, the sprawling carriage works on the outskirts of the railway town of Wolverton, the excavated remains of a Roman villa and a restored windmill combine to provide an excellent walk, packed with interest.

The Walk

From the New Inn the route turns left, down and over the Grand Union canal bridge and left again, down steps leading to the towpath. After a bend the canal crosses above the dual carriageway of the main road via the Grafton Street Aqueduct, the first new aqueduct to be built on the canal system for 50 years.

From here the canal is followed as it heads west, across the city, and eventually, after passing under a railway bridge, British Rail's works are passed on the opposite bank. The perimeter wall facing the canal has a black on white train mural at least 100 yards long. Beyond the works a road bridge is first passed under before the route turns sharply right, to climb steps up to the road. Wolverton main-line railway station is below to the left as the route turns right, across the bridge over the canal. Across the road on the other side of the bridge a path on the left leads down steps, back to the towpath, now on the opposite side of the canal. From here a path follows the canal back past the railway works before bending left, on a subway under the railway line. A hundred yards or so further on, the path leaves the canal as it bears away to the right through bushes and meets a Redway path. Here, it turns right and follows the Redway through the Blue Bridge housing estate. Over a first service road, it continues ahead before turning left, under the main road, on a pedestrian underpass. From here it runs downhill through more houses and across another service road, just beyond which the line of

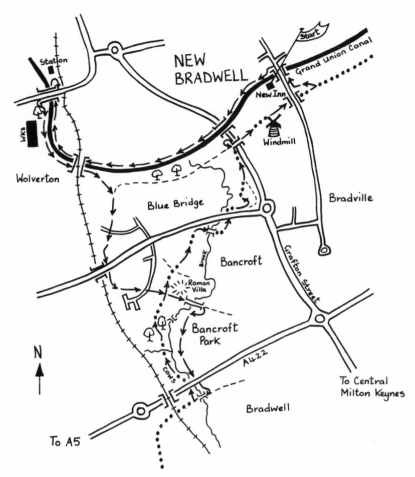

the Midshires Way/Swan's Way is crossed. (A short-cut is available by turning left here on to the long-distance path – see map.)

Across the line of the long-distance path, the main pub walk continues ahead, down past the excavated foundations of a Roman villa which once stood on the slopes of the valley. Three large display boards give details of the history of this site which dates back many centuries. Past here a long wooden footbridge crosses a marshy area at the bottom of the valley followed by a first crossing of Loughton Brook. At the end of the bridge, the route turns right, down steps leading to a gravelled path. Here it turns left, along the path which keeps to the left of the stream along the valley bottom. After a short distance the concrete cows can be seen on the opposite bank, but the path keeps ahead, under the main road. Across a footbridge over the stream to the right the pub walk turns

49

right and joins the Midshires Way/Swan's Way.

From here the path runs back under the main road and past the famous concrete cows donated to the town in 1978, by Liz Leyh. As sculptures, the cows are idiosyncratic to say the least but, love them or hate them, they are now identified with Milton Keynes and have become an inseparable part of its landscape.

Past here the route stays with the path as it bends right and left over streams and round ponds through a more wooded area of Bancroft Park. Clear of the trees it continues ahead, across the line of the path walked earlier, with the outline remains of the Roman villa now below to the right. Another information board with details of the villa is passed after which the route keeps ahead at a junction on a path which bends right, along the base of a road embankment. It bends right again, across a bridge over the stream, then the route turns left and follows a path under the main road. Having passed under the road, the path bends right, then left (the riders' route diverges to the right), before bending right again, and running up to the main road. The road is followed for a short distance as the path runs down to and under a footbridge, immediately beyond which it turns sharply left, up to the bridge. Across the bridge, which parallels the aqueduct crossed earlier, there is a remarkable view of the narrow boats as they float high above the dual carriageway.

On the other side of the bridge the route continues ahead on Railway Walk, to the right of which is Bradwell Windmill, built in 1816. A view board in front of the mill gives full details of its history. The route follows the dismantled railway line and passes under a road bridge, on the other side of which it leaves the Midshires Way as it turns sharply left, back up to the road.

At the road the walk turns right, back down to the New Inn.

Midshires Way - New Bradwell to Great Linford (1 mile)
From the concrete cows the route is described in detail as far as the railway bridge, New Bradwell (see above). From here the route stays with the Swan's Way along the dismantled railway known as Railway Walk. Opposite Stantonbury Underpass it bears left, down to and along the bridletrack which follows the line of the embankment as far as the Grand Union canal. Here, it turns left, along the towpath. Past the pub on the opposite bank, it crosses over a road bridge and turns left, back down to the canal. Beyond here the route is described in Pub Walk 10, from the Black Horse, Great Linford (Milton Keynes).

[10] Great Linford
The Black Horse

Great Linford now lies within the northern boundary of Milton Keynes and its name probably derives from the name of the crossing point over the river Great Ouse where there were lime (or linden) trees.

The Black Horse is located to the north-west of the village, on the Grand Union canal. An inn has stood here for many centuries, long before the canal was built. An attractive, rambling building, much altered over the centuries, its spacious and heavily beamed interior now provides accommodation on a number of levels, each with its own style. Brasses, 'roses and castles' decorated narrow boat ware and old canal photographs abound in the two bars in which a large, open fireplace adds character and comfort in the winter. In addition to the bars, the various split levels overlooking the canal are interlinked to provide a restaurant and a servery/non-smoking area. An open-ended upstairs room allows a flexible extension of the accommodation, whether for dining or semi-private parties. It is also occasionally used by drama companies who travel the canals in narrow boats and perform Victorian melodramas at canal-side venues.

Home cooking includes traditional dishes such as hearty soups, steak and kidney pie made to an old English recipe, home-cooked ham, egg and chips. In addition, chalkboard specials include freshly prepared dishes of the day, such as beef in red wine or prawn piri-piri. There is also a vegetarian choice and a children's menu. Meals are available seven days a week, but it is advisable to book in advance at weekends or bank holidays when demand is heavy.

There is a large, canal-side garden to the rear of the pub, complete with small stage for summer entertainments. A weekend barbecue adds the finishing touch to the attractions of this very popular pub.

The Black Horse is an Ind Coope establishment and serves their ABC Best Bitter and Burton Ale, plus Tetley Bitter. Three lagers and a cider are also available on draught.

The opening times are Monday to Saturday from 11 am to 11 pm, and on Sunday from 12 noon to 10.30 pm.

Telephone: 01908 605939.

How to get there: Great Linford is 1 mile west of Newport Pagnell, on the northern edge of Milton Keynes. Turn off the A422 between the M1 and the A5 for Stantonbury or Great Linford. The pub is signposted off the Wolverton road on the northern side of the Grand Union canal.

Parking: There is a large car park in front of the pub.

Length of the walk: 4 miles. Map: OS Landranger 152 Northampton and Milton Keynes (inn GR 847424).

From the canal this walk explores a watery landscape of rivers and lakes. An ideal opportunity to get away from it all, right on the northern doorstep of this new town.

The Walk

From the rear of the Black Horse the route turns right, along the towpath of the Grand Union canal. Apart from travelling players, narrow boat shops sometimes moor here, selling a glittering array of decorative ware and canal paraphernalia. Under the nearby road bridge, the walk is joined by the Midshires/Swan's Way.

The walk continues along the towpath past narrow boats used as houseboats before leaving the canal as it turns right, through a waymarked five-bar metal gate. From here a metalled track crosses a cattle grid and runs down and across the Great Ouse valley with the first of many lakes on the right. Extensive gravel workings in this low lying area have resulted in the formation of lakes with beneficial effects for both leisure and wildlife. The building down by the edge of the lake to the right is a private wildfowl centre and one of the lakes is used for water sports.

Down in the valley the track follows a stone wall as it turns left for

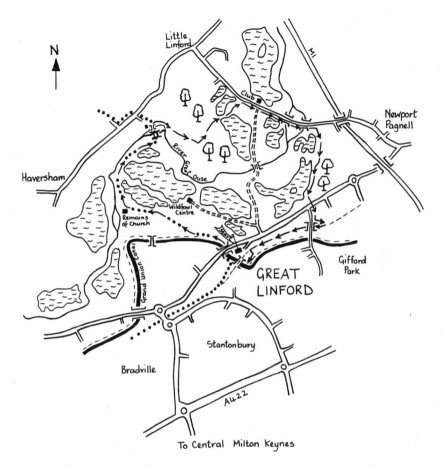

some distance before bearing right, opposite the ancient ruins of the one-time parish church of Stantonbury.

Further along the track bears right and then continues ahead, sandwiched between the river Great Ouse and lakes on the right. This particular stretch across open pastures provides an ideal chance to observe the numerous birds and waterfowl on the lake and the river. Eventually, the track turns left and crosses a bridge over the river at Haversham Weir, after which the track becomes a farm access road. Past a cottage, farm buildings and a stone barn, it goes through a gate and the pub walk leaves the Midshires Way.

Here, the walk turns right, across to a fingerpost from which it turns sharply right, across a meadow and through an open gateway. Keeping ahead up the rise, it bears left, past the corner of the field on the same

53

side and across to a stile and continues in the same direction to another stile on the corner of a wood. From here the route bears left, following wooden posts across open ground with more lakes on the right. The path then leads through trees to emerge on a causeway between two lakes, with excellent views across the water on both sides. Where the causeway ends, a stile next to a gate takes the path through a plantation of young broad-leaved and coniferous trees, then past a bullrush-lined smaller lake. At a small car park, the route turns right, along a narrow lane and soon passes Dovecote Lake Water Sports Centre on the left. During the summer and at weekends, the club house and bar are open to the public for refreshments, which can be enjoyed sitting at the lake-side picnic tables.

With lakes now on both sides, the lane continues across two bridges over the Great Ouse before turning right, on a bridletrack just before the Newport Pagnell sign. Keeping to the left of a gate, it follows a fence before bending right to a wooden swing-gate through which it turns left, along the banks of a tree-lined lake. At another gate the route turns left, and runs up to and across a main road before bearing right, along the front of Station Terrace. It then turns left, along the road to Great Linford which is followed up to just before the old railway bridge. Here the route turns left on a path down to the dismantled railway line and right, along Railway Walk. Under the road bridge the metalled path on the raised embankment provides easy, relaxed walking until, just before the bridge over the canal, the route turns left, down steps to the canal towpath. Here, it turns right, and follows the canal under the railway bridge beyond which it is only a short distance back to the Black Horse.

Midshires Way – Great Linford to Hartwell (8 miles)

From here an alternative route for walkers would be to stay with the canal, instead of trekking across country in company with horses, and rejoin the Midshires Way at Blisworth (Pub Walk 13).

However, the official route continues to follow the Swan's Way and is described in detail up to and across the Great Ouse river (see above). From here a farm road leads up to a lane along which it turns left, then right, on a track heading northwards across farming uplands. After clipping Linford Wood, it keeps to the right of the aerial complex at Hanslope to another minor road along which it turns right. At Tathall End (B&B available at Woad Farm, telephone: 01908 510985), it leaves the road to follow a track under the M1 and keeps roughly parallel with the motorway before crossing arable fields to enter Salcey Forest. At the road it turns left and crosses the county border, beyond which the route is described in Pub Walk 11 from the Rose and Crown, Hartwell.

[11] Hartwell
The Rose and Crown

Hartwell is a small village on the western fringes of Salcey Forest, once a royal hunting ground.

The Rose and Crown is an attractive country pub, close to the centre of the village. Built as an inn in 1726, it originally served the coaching and carriage trade and today has built up a reputation in the area for good food at very reasonable prices. The interior has been recently refurbished and wooden beams, exposed brickwork and open fireplaces create a countrified atmosphere. A long bar serves an open-plan L-shaped area, comfortably furnished and carpeted throughout, with wheel-back chairs and separate tables for dining. Home-made, traditional pub grub offers very good value for money and includes all the usual favourites, such as steak and kidney or rabbit pies, plus a selection of soups, curries and chillies. Sunday roast is considered a house speciality and booking in advance is advisable. 'Specials' always include vegetarian dishes, children are catered for and meals are available seven days a week.

Real ales on offer include Webster's Yorkshire Bitter, Draught Bass and Gale's Pompey Royal. Guinness, cider and three lagers are also available on draught. There is a separate games and pool room, plus a pleasant garden to the rear of the pub.

The opening times are Monday to Saturday from 11.30 am to 2.30 pm and 6.30 pm to 11 pm, and on Sunday from 12 noon to 3 pm and 7 pm to 10.30 pm.

Telephone: 01604 862393.

How to get there: Hartwell lies west of the M1, just inside Northamptonshire, 6 miles north of Milton Keynes. From the M1 (J15), take the A508 south, or from the A5 take the A508 north, to Roade and then minor roads to the village. The pub is at the centre of the village.

Parking: There is a large car park to the rear of the pub.

Length of the walk: 3 miles (longer options possible). Map: OS Landranger 152 Northampton and Milton Keynes (inn GR 786504).

A walk in Salcey Forest, now owned by the Forestry Commission. The forest is managed not only to produce timber but also to provide and protect wildlife habitat. An ideal woodland walk, especially for 'twitchers' or those with an interest in natural history and conservation.

The Walk

From the car park at the rear of the pub, the route turns left and follows the path to the corner of the field. Over a stile it runs along the bottom of the gardens before another stile and fenced path leads to a road (Malting Way). A roadside path is followed up to the T-junction where the route turns right. Where the road ends the route continues ahead along a bridleway track which passes a playing field on the left, then keeps to the left of the hedge as more open country is reached. At a gap in the hedge ahead the route turns left, and follows the hedge down to the bottom corner of the field. Here, a footbridge takes the route left, through a small wood before turning left again along the bottom of the motorway embankment. At a service road it turns right, under the M1, on the other side of which it turns left, past the end of a metal gate, on the fringes of Salcey Forest.

Just inside the gate a path on the right, marked 'permit horse trail', takes the route into the forest and away from the motorway. The path continues ahead through broad-leaved woodland and over grassy rides which provide an ideal habitat for butterflies and wildlife. The route crosses straight over a minor road and continues along a broad track for some distance before turning left. Along this stretch the forest is divided with fir tree plantations to the left, and broad-leaved trees to the right. Past a forestry worker's house on the right, the track meets the road opposite the main entrance to Salcey Lawn, an open, grassy area once managed to provide hay and pasture for deer.

Here the pub walk joins the Midshires Way as it turns left, along the road. Eventually, it crosses straight over a crossroads and leaves the long-distance route which turns right.

At this point, the pub walk can be extended by turning right, with the Midshires Way. A short distance along the road, from a car park and picnic area on the right, the Forestry Commission offers a choice of two 'Woodpecker Trails' and a chance to explore more of the forest.

The main pub walk, however, having kept ahead over the crossroads, crosses over the M1 motorway and follows a roadside path through the village, back to the Rose and Crown.

Midshires Way – Hartwell to Roade (7 miles)

Having crossed the county border, the road is followed up to the crossroads where it turns right (see above). From here it runs past

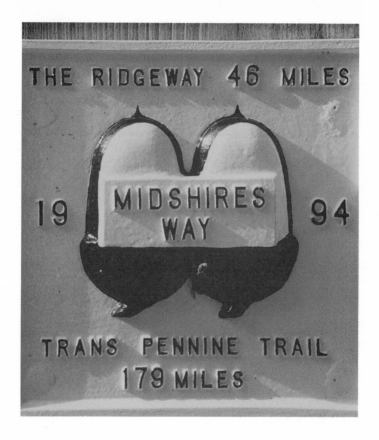

the main car park and picnic area in Salcey Forest. A bridleway on
the right takes it for about 1 mile just inside the edge of the forest
before turning left to emerge onto open, arable farmland. The route
turns right for some distance, then left, along a hedged byway which
crosses a dismantled railway line and continues almost up to the village
of Piddington. Just past the farm buildings it turns left again on a track
heading west for 2 miles across arable farmland. From the road at the
southern end of Quinton Green (B&B available at Quinton Green Farm,
telephone: 01604 863685), it follows field paths to a footbridge over the
M1. Over the motorway it turns right for several fields, then left, up to
and down the left-hand (eastern) side of Fox Covert. It then continues
ahead before turning right at the bridleway junction just past the line
of the disused railway. The hedge is followed to the road where the
route turns right, into the village of Roade. Beyond here it is described
in Pub Walk 12 from the Cock, Roade.

[12] Roade
The Cock

Roade is bisected by a deep railway cutting carved from almost solid rock which, when it opened to rail traffic in 1838, was the largest man-made cutting in the world.

The Cock is located on the eastern side of the village, near a small green and war memorial. A large, rambling building originally built as a farmhouse in 1750, its spacious interior allows for two separate bars, a long, L-shaped lounge, and a public bar with games such as skittles. The bright and cheerful lounge provides a warm, welcoming atmosphere in which brasses gleam in the light of the open fire. The pub advertises itself as 'the happy little mad place' and the couple who run it make everyone feel very welcome. A range of home-made meals on offer includes soups, or appetizers such as calamares Romana, (battered squid served with salad and dip), to grilled steaks or the ever popular steak, mushroom and Guinness pie. Vegetarian choice includes such dishes as vegetable tikka masala or pasta Alfredo, 'a piping hot bowl of pasta, sliced mushrooms, broccoli, cauliflower florets, cream and basil'. Meals are not served on Sunday evenings or Tuesday lunchtimes. There is a garden to one side of the pub and well-behaved dogs on a lead are welcome in the bars.

The Cock is a freehouse and real ales on offer include Theakston

Best Bitter, Theakston XB, Hall and Woodhouse Tanglefoot, Timothy Chudley, Buchanan's 80/- and Gale's HSB. Youngers Best Bitter, Guinness, cider and three lagers are also available on draught.

The notice outside the main door regarding opening and the availability of the landlord sets the tone of this hostelry, but the official opening times are Monday to Saturday from 11 am to 3 pm and 6 pm to 11 pm, and on Sunday from 12 noon to 3 pm and 7 pm to 10.30 pm.

Telephone: 01604 862544.

How to get there: Roade lies between the A43 and the M1, 6 miles south of Northampton on the A508. Take the A508 from J15 of the M1 south, or the A508 north from the A5 at Old Stratford. The pub is on the eastern side of the village at the end of the High Street.

Parking: There is a large car park to one side of the pub.

Length of the walk: 5 miles. Map: OS Landranger 152 Northampton and Milton Keynes (inn GR 759517).

A walk across high, rolling farmland to the Stoke Bruerne end of the Blisworth Tunnel on the Grand Union canal. From here a short stretch of towpath leads to the village of Stoke Bruerne itself with its interesting museum and the canal-side Boat Inn.

The Walk

From the pub, which lies on the Midshires Way, the route turns left, down the High Street. Past the Leys on the left, the pub walk follows an interesting diversion off the long-distance route as it turns right, up Church End to the ancient church of St Mary the Virgin. A cycle path is followed past the church and up to a green where the walk turns left, along a path and track between houses to the main road. Here the long-distance route is rejoined as the walk dog-legs to the right across the road, down Hyde Road. After crossing a railway bridge, the road bends to the right, but the walk continues ahead following a track to Hyde Farm. The track becomes a path to the right of a fence and more open farmland is reached across which headland tracks continue in a generally westward direction. There are good views across the mainly arable farmland to the south and, eventually, a hedged track leads to a narrow lane. Here, the Midshires Way crosses straight over, but the pub walk turns left.

To the right, in front of a cluster of farm buildings, a ventilation tower is the first indication of the proximity of the Blisworth Tunnel. After a short distance the lane bears right, but the walk continues ahead through a metal gate to follow a good track along which a horse tramway once

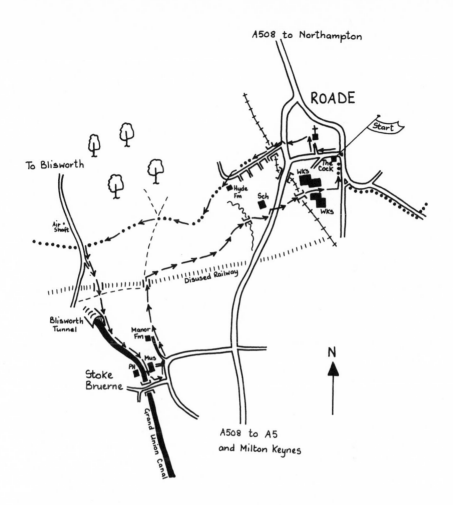

connected each side of the hill while the tunnel was under construction. The track crosses a dismantled railway line and eventually runs down to the Grand Union canal and the southern entrance to the Blisworth Tunnel. Originally completed in 1805, the tunnel was restored and reopened in 1984 and, at 1³/₄ miles, is the longest navigable tunnel in the country. From here the route follows the canal towpath for a short distance before arriving at Stoke Bruerne where the Boat Inn, in its appealing, canal-side setting, adds to the interest of the canal museum and shop.

At the road bridge, the route leaves the canal as it turns left, along the road to the T-junction. Here it turns left again, and as the road bends right, continues ahead along Mill Lane. After the houses and the lane ends a wide, hedged track continues ahead. Past the remains of another railway bridge the route bears diagonally right, across a small pasture to a stile over which a path continues ahead, bearing left across an arable field. Through a gap in the hedge, it keeps to the right of a line of oak trees, at the end of which the path crosses another arable field, keeping well to the left of the opposite corner. Over another stile the path runs down a pasture (aim for the school buildings ahead), to a footbridge over which it crosses a grassy ride. Over another stile it turns right, following the fence. At the bottom of the bank on the edge of the school's playing field, the path turns right. In the corner, just before reaching the road, it turns left and continues to follow the edge of the playing field in front of the school. After 50 yards or so it turns right, through the hedge to emerge on the roadside path just before the village signs for Roade.

Here, it turns left and, past the signs and the main entrance to the school, crosses to the other side of the road at a traffic sign, down a driveway or entrance to the right of a hedge. Past the end of some warehouses a tarmaced path runs to a footbridge over the railway line across which it continues ahead through a complex of factory buildings. Eventually, it emerges on the road along which the walk turns left, past the war memorial and back to the Cock.

Midshires Way – Roade to Blisworth (3½ miles)

From Roade, the route is described in detail as far as the lane over the Blisworth Tunnel (see above). From here the route follows a bridletrack which, after passing a small pond, veers to the right along the hedgeline. Just before reaching Nun Wood it turns right, through a gate onto a track known as Nun Lane, which is followed north. From a bridletrack on the left before the tunnel entrance, the route is described in Pub Walk 13, from the Royal Oak, Blisworth.

B&B is available at the Blisworth Hotel, telephone: 01604 859551; camping is available at the Royal Oak, Blisworth, telephone: 01604 858372.

[13] Blisworth
The Royal Oak

Blisworth lies a short distance from the entrance to the canal tunnel that takes its name, the other end of which, over 1 mile away, was visited in the previous pub walk.

Some of the older cottages in the village are thatched and built of contrasting courses of the local ironstone and sandstone. The Royal Oak, built on the top of the small hill near the centre of the village, lost its thatched roof in a fire in 1958, although the main building escaped serious damage. Built as an inn in the 17th century, today it is a popular stop for leisure craft on the nearby canal and well known by the locals for its good value home cooking and well kept beer. Two interconnected bars, a huge ingle-nook fireplace and heavy beams combine to create the feeling of a homely, country inn. Accommodation extends to a separate games and pool room. Traditional pub grub includes large Yorkshire puddings with a range of fillings from steak and kidney to game casserole. Those in search of something more exotic should try the highly recommended chicken curry prepared to an authentic, Yorkshire, recipe! There is a choice of vegetarian dishes and meals are served seven days a week. There is a large garden complete with dovecote to the rear of the pub. With room to spare, the landlord is amenable to overnight camping on the grassy area next to the garden.

Real ales on offer include John Smith's Bitter and Magnet, Boddingtons Bitter, Courage Directors, and Morland Old Speckled Hen. Whitbread Trophy, Guinness, three lagers and a cider are also available on draught.

The opening hours are Monday to Saturday from 11 am to 3.30 pm and 5.30 pm to 11 pm, and on Sunday from 12 noon to 3 pm and 7 pm to 10.30 pm.

Telephone: 01604 858372.

How to get there: Blisworth lies between the M1 and the A43(T), just 4 miles south-west of Northampton. Turn off the A43(T) midway between J15(a) of the M1 and the A5, or turn off the A508 near Roade to follow signposted C roads. The pub is at the centre of the village.

Parking: There is a good-sized car park to one side of the pub.

Length of the walk: 3 miles (longer option possible). Map: OS Landranger 152 Northampton and Milton Keynes (inn GR 727535).

An easy walk through the village and across open farmland via the entrance to the Blisworth Tunnel, the longest navigable tunnel in the country. From here the walk is full of canal-side interest as it follows the Grand Union canal towpath back to the village.

The Walk

From the Royal Oak the route turns right, down the High Street past the church of St John the Baptist, built of local limestone and ironstone. Past the derelict Sun, Moon and Stars, the road reaches the bottom of the hill, where it crosses a bridge over the Grand Union canal next to a Victorian, red-brick mill (Westley Mill). Beyond the mill Blisworth Tunnel Boats Ltd have established a hire-fleet of narrow boats, a repair dock, chandlery and moorings, all of which make the bridge an excellent place from which to observe boating business below.

Past the bridge, the walk takes the left-hand road signposted to Towcester along a roadside path. At the top of a long rise, just past the end of the line of houses on the left, the route turns left, on a bridleway signposted to Shutlanger. After passing silos and a barn, it turns left, just before a farm entrance gate, along a grassy, hedged track. Where the hedges end, it continues ahead as a headland track across several fields before passing through a metal gate to join the Midshires Way.

From here it turns diagonally left, in company with the long-distance route, and keeps to the left of a stream down a narrow pasture. To the right can be seen one of the seven brick-built air shafts

64

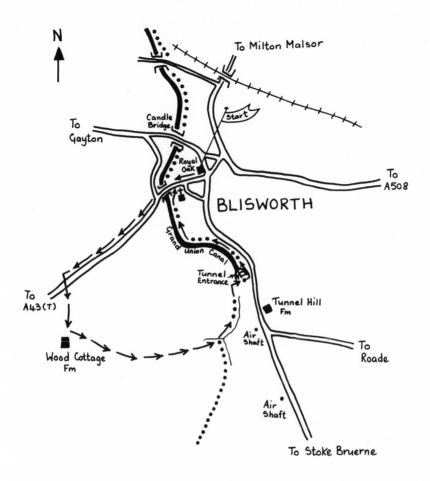

which were built in the 19th century along the line of the Blisworth Tunnel. Through a swing-gate, the walk continues ahead down pastures and through another gate where it turns right, along a track. Just before the nearby road is reached it turns left, on a path which runs down the embankment to reach the Grand Union canal to the right of the tunnel entrance. The air shafts referred to above were built following the introduction of steam tugs in 1871. Prior to this, boats were 'legged' through the tunnel by men who lay on their backs on special boards and pushed the boat forward by 'walking' the tunnel sides – a dark, laborious process that took up to three hours.

The route turns right, along the towpath and, eventually, a bend in the canal reveals the bridge crossed earlier at the bottom of Blisworth High Street. Here the pub walk leaves the Midshires Way as it turns right, up

The Grand Union Canal at Blisworth.

the embankment to the road.

From here the route is retraced, back up the hill to the pub, although the walk can be extended along to the next bridge on the canal, where the road to the right also leads back to the Royal Oak.

Midshires Way – Blisworth to Nether Heyford (6½ miles)

From the bridletrack before the tunnel entrance the route is described in detail as far as Blisworth (see above). From here the route stays with the canal and, after passing under the main-line railway bridge, a slight detour away from the canal takes it past Gayton Junction, where the Northampton arm joins the canal. Eventually, after the road bridge into Bugbrooke, the route is described in Pub Walk 14, from the Olde Sun, Nether Heyford.

B&B is available at 27 Church Street, Nether Heyford, telephone: 01327 340872.

[14] Nether Heyford
The Olde Sun

Nether Heyford is in the Nene Valley and its outskirts border the Grand Union canal. The centre of the village has a 5–acre green, to the north of which stands the village church in the older part of the village.

The Olde Sun was built of local stone over 400 years ago, since when it has served as the village inn. It is a large building whose spacious interior is remarkable not so much for its size, as for its contents. Outside, restored and brightly painted beet crushers and a collection of enamelled tin signs only hint at the mind-boggling collection of memorabilia within. An orderly riot of copper kettles, brass scales, shell cases, diver's helmets, clocks, butter churns, earthenware jugs, wall plaques and wood carvings, plus numerous unidentifiable bits and pieces, festoon the ceilings, walls and fireplaces in the two bars. The first bar has one end reserved for skittles and darts, whilst a mixture of upholstered settles with individual tables and chairs comfortably furnish the rest. Exposed stonework and a huge ingle-nook fireplace add the final touches to this bar. The second, or inner, bar is a snug on the grand scale, with split level seating, another open fireplace, and a bar that gleams invitingly at one end.

A separate dining-room, on yet another level, serves a good range of home-cooked meals, including soups, char-grilled steaks, local ham, egg and chips, chicken stir-fry and fresh battered cod. The blackboard menu changes daily and traditional Sunday lunches are so popular that it is advisable to book in advance. There is always a selection of vegetarian dishes and children's portions are available. Meals are not served at lunchtimes on a Monday.

There is a large, walled garden to the rear of the pub. Well behaved dogs on a leash are allowed in the bars, but not the dining-room. Dry boots are acceptable, muddy boots are not.

The Olde Sun is a freehouse and serves the following cask conditioned real ales – Theakston Best Bitter, Webster's Yorkshire Bitter, John Smith's Bitter, Banks's Bitter and Courage Directors. Guinness, cider and three lagers are also available on draught.

The opening times are, Monday, evening only from 6 pm to 11 pm; Tuesday to Friday, 12 noon to 2 pm and 6 pm to 11 pm; Saturday, 12 noon to 3 pm and 6 pm to 11 pm and Sunday, 12 noon to 3 pm and 7 pm to 10.30 pm.

Telephone: 01327 340164.

How to get there: Nether Heyford lies between the M1 and the A5, just 5 miles west of Northampton. From the M1, take the A45 (to Daventry), and turn off on a C road signposted from Upper Heyford, or turn off the A5, between Weedon Bec and Pattishall. The pub is north of the village green on Middle Street, near the school.

Parking: There is a car park to one side of the pub.

Length of the walk: 5 miles. Map: OS Landranger 152 Northampton and Milton Keynes (inn GR 662586).

A walk along the valley and the Nene Way to the village of Bugbrooke. The return leg incorporates easy walking along the Grand Union canal, alive with boating business during the summer months.

The Walk
From the Olde Sun the route turns right, along the road for a short distance before turning right again, along a fenced footpath signposted for the Nene Way. At Watery Lane it dog-legs across to the right and continues to follow the Nene Way along a track also signposted for Kislingbury and Bugbrooke. Past playing fields on the left, the walk clears the village as it crosses a stream and bears left on a grassy headland track. At the corner of the field it turns left, then right, to follow a headland path with good views across open countryside to higher ground to the north. Over a footbridge and stile, the route continues ahead over

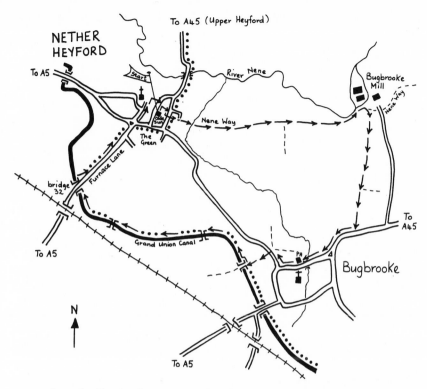

a series of stiles in the corner of mainly arable fields before reaching a
track to the right of a bridge over the river Nene. Across the other side
of the river can be seen the vast, rumbling complex of Heygates Mill, the
headquarters of England's largest independent millers.

Keeping ahead to the right of the river, the track leads to a tarmaced
farm road along which it turns left, following the river past the front
of the mill. The road then bears away from the river and, at a wooden
gate, the route parts company with the Nene Way as it turns right, on
a footpath across an arable field. Over the field, a headland path keeps
to the left of the hedge which is followed up and over rising ground.
Two stiles and a short stretch of path lead to a road on the outskirts of
Bugbrooke along which the route turns right. At the junction past the
village hall it turns right, down Church Lane. After passing the church
of St Michael and All Angels opposite the Five Bells, it turns right again
at a T-junction. After a few hundred yards it turns left, on a metalled
track which runs down to the Grand Union canal. At the canal bridge
a path on the right-hand side leads down the embankment to the canal
towpath.

The walk now joins the Midshires Way as it turns right, along the towpath, for a good mile of easy, pleasant, canal-side walking. At bridge number 32 the route parts company with the Grand Union canal for the last time. Under the bridge a path on the right leads up to Furnace Lane, so-called because three blast furnaces once operated in the area between here and the railway. The route turns left along this now quiet, minor road. After passing through more recent housing on the outskirts of Nether Heyford the lane crosses one of the largest village greens in England. At the crossroads the pub walk keeps ahead, but the Midshires Way turns right.

Having crossed over the crossroads, the walk follows the road through the oldest part of the village. Where the road bends left, it continues ahead on a no-through road to the right of the 12th century village church. Where the road ends, it turns right, along the Nene Way again, which is followed to the road. Here, the route turns right, back to the Olde Sun.

Midshires Way – Nether Heyford to Nobottle (3 miles)

From the canal bridge outside Bugbrooke, the route is described in detail as far as the green in Nether Heyford (see above). At the crossroads, it turns right and then takes the second left, along Watery Lane. After crossing the line of the Nene Way it continues to the end of the lane where the route turns right. Over the river Nene, the lane is followed to Upper Heyford on the A45. A tarmac track leads off the main road to a bridge over the M1, which is crossed for the last time. From here an unsurfaced track runs north, over undulating, open countryside. Through several gates the route continues up rising ground before crossing over a stream just before a rifle-range. From here the route is described in Pub Walk 15 from the Fox and Hounds, Great Brington.

[15] Great Brington
The Fox and Hounds

Great Brington is a very attractive village, best known for its proximity to Althorp House, the ancestral home of the Spencer family and the Princess of Wales. The 13th century village church has a Spencer chapel and the family has been a power in the county over the centuries.

The Fox and Hounds is a large, thatched building, built around 1765, which now styles itself as 'The Althorp Coaching Inn' – a coaching arch and stables on one side of a cobbled yard testify to its past history, if not its present claim. Inside, flagstones, bare boards and quarry tiles together with wooden settles and traditional farmhouse furniture combine to create a rural style which deliberately disdains such fripperies as carpets and curtains. A collection of agricultural paraphernalia adorns the walls whilst a stuffed parrot in a large bird-cage suspended from the ceiling keeps a beady eye on the clientele. A horse-shoe shaped bar serves interconnected areas on various levels in which an informal ambience inspires genial conviviality.

In addition to bar meals, such as mussels in real ale, rabbit stew and pigeon pie, the 'Hobson's Choice' menu in the cellar restaurant allows a choice of anything as long as it's home-made pies. Six varieties are on offer including local game pie and fish. Vegetarians have a choice and

71

home-made sweets include such delights as jam roly poly and spotted dick. Meals are available seven days a week.

There is a very pleasant garden to the rear of the pub, complete with a barbecue at weekends during the summer months. In keeping with its relaxed style the Fox and Hounds has adopted the motto, 'You'll never want to leave' – I'll drink to that!

In addition to all its other attractions, the pub has a fine selection of real ales, including Gibbs Mew Bishop's Tipple, Brakspear Bitter, Bateman Victory Ale, Morland Old Speckled Hen, Theakston Old Peculier, Theakston XB, Marston's Pedigree Bitter, Wadworth 6X, Timothy Taylor Landlord, Jennings Cumberland Ale, Eldridge Pope Indian Summer, and a local brew called Old Gun Dog.

The opening times are Monday to Friday from 12 noon to 3 pm and 5 pm to 11 pm; on Saturday, noon to 11 pm and on Sunday, 12 noon to 3 pm and 7 pm to 10.30 pm.

Telephone: 01604 770651.

How to get there: Great Brington lies 5 miles north-west of Northampton between the M1 and the A428. Turn off the A428 (Northampton-Rugby) at Harlestone or East Haddon and follow C roads, or, from the M1 (J16), take the A45 to Flore and then follow signposted C roads to the village. The pub is in the centre, next to the post office.

Parking: There is a large car park behind the pub.

Length of the walk: 5 miles (shorter option possible). Map: OS Landranger 152 Northampton and Milton Keynes (inn GR 666649).

A walk via Little Brington with wide views across open countryside to the south. After descending from the ridge, it runs back up to the hamlet of Nobottle and across farming uplands with views now to the north and occasional glimpses of Althorp House in its parkland setting.

The Walk

From the pub the route turns right, along the road. Beyond the last of the thatched cottages it stays with the roadside path until just past a seat on the right. Here a path on the same side leaves the road and skirts old stone workings as it heads diagonally left, across a pasture. Over a footbridge and stiles it follows the same direction across an arable field to another stile from which it bears left. Two more pastures followed by a double stile take it between houses and up to the road to the right of the Saracen's Head, Little Brington.

Here, the short-cut turns left (see sketch map), but the main pub

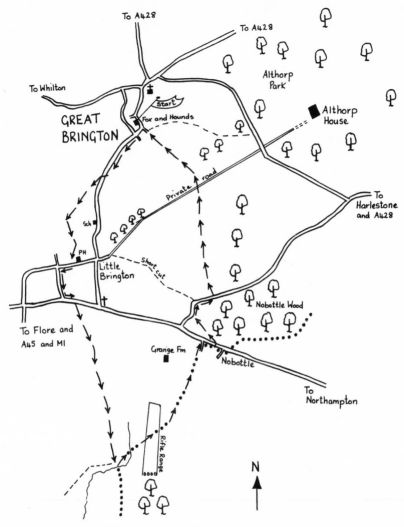

walk turns right. The road is followed to a crossroads just past an old farmyard, where it turns left. From here a narrow lane runs up to the main road across which the route turns left, up to a lay-by. Ahead on the left-hand side of the road can be seen the spire of the former church of St John, built in 1856 by the 4th Earl Spencer. After the Second World War the church fell into disuse and was only saved from complete demolition at the request of the Air Ministry, since the tower was a familiar landmark to RAF pilots.

At the lay-by the route turns right, down a track which is, in fact, an

73

unsurfaced country road which runs down from the ridge with mainly arable fields to the right and sheep pastures to the left. As the track flattens out it continues ahead across pleasant, open countryside and eventually arrives at a metal farm gate. Through this the route keeps to the left of the hedge and at the bottom corner of this field, it picks up the Midshires Way.

From here the return leg turns sharply left, crossing the corner of the field to a gateway on the boundary of a rarely used rifle-range. Diagonally left across another pasture, a gate takes the walk across the range with the butts clearly visible at the base of the hill on the right. A track on the edge of the range is crossed to another gate, through which another on the left leads to a wide, hedged track. Eventually, the track becomes a metalled lane past the thatched cottages in the hamlet of Nobottle, where it meets the road crossed earlier. Here, the route turns right, along the road and crosses to a fingerpost on the left where the pub walk leaves the Midshires Way.

From the fingerpost a path cuts across the bottom corner of the field as it crosses diagonally left through an open gateway at the corner of a wood. It then continues up and over a small hill to a roadside stile in the top right-hand corner of the field. Over this the route turns right, along the lane which it stays with round the first bend, where the short-cut comes in on the left. Further along the lane, just before Nobottle Wood is reached, the route turns left, on a footpath prominently signposted to Great Brington. From here the path runs ahead over a wide sheep pasture with good views of Great Brington ahead, before running down across two arable fields and over the private road to Althorp House. Across a last arable field, the path bears left over wide pastures, aiming roughly for the centre of the village. Three stiles are crossed over rising ground with good views of Althorp House to the right. Through a gate a concrete drive becomes a lane which leads between houses to the road walked earlier, where the route turns right, back to the Fox and Hounds.

Midshires Way – Nobottle to Lower Harlestone (2 miles)

From just before the rifle-range, the route is described in detail as far as Nobottle (see above). Here it turns right, along the road, and leaves on a bridleway to the left, just past the green. It then turns right along the edge of Nobottle Wood before heading north-east across arable farmland to Harlestone. Here, the route turns left, down a lane to meet the road through the village, along which it turns right. The walkers' route leaves the road on the left along paths and tracks leading to Lower Harlestone where it turns right on the A428. From here the route is described in Pub Walk 16 from the Fox and Hounds, Lower Harlestone.

[16] Lower Harlestone
The Fox and Hounds

The Harlestones, Upper and Lower, contain many attractive houses and estate cottages built of the local warm brown sandstone. The Fox and Hounds is a substantial hostelry dating from the early 1700s, whose name reflects a strong tradition of hunting in this part of the county. Inside, there are two separate bars, the larger of which, the Pytchley, celebrates the locally famous hunt. Wooden beams and exposed stonework create a rural atmosphere whilst the split levels in the lounge bar combine with the ingle nook fireplace to create an inviting cosiness. The pub is well-known for its value-for-money home cooking and has a wide selection of traditional pub food ranging from pies to steaks, curries and chillis, plus a vegetarian selection. Blackboard specials include hotpots and steak and kidney pies, followed by sweets such as apple pie and fruit crumble. As a very popular venue for business lunches, it is advisable to phone in advance during the week. Meals are not served on Sundays, or on a Monday evening. There is a garden to the rear of the pub in which a fairly large, open-sided, wooden building provides protection from the average English summer. Dogs are welcome in the garden.

Real ales served at the Fox and Hounds include Wadworth 6X, John Smith's Bitter, Marston's Pedigree Bitter and Tetley Bitter. Beamish,

Guinness, cider and four lagers are also available on draught.

The opening times are Monday to Saturday from 11 am to 3 pm and 5.30 pm to 11 pm, and on Sunday from 12 noon to 3 pm and 7 pm to 10.30 pm.

Telephone: 01604 843334.

How to get there: Lower Harlestone lies on the A428, just 3 miles north-west of Northampton. The pub is on the main road, towards the south-eastern end of the village.

Parking: There is a small car park to one side of the pub plus another much larger one to the rear.

Length of the walk: 4 miles. Map: OS Landranger 152 Northampton and Milton Keynes (inn GR 707645).

A pleasant, easy walk which follows the Midshires Way across the sandy tracks of Harlestone Heath, returning via Church Brampton golf course.

The Walk

From the Fox and Hounds the route turns left, along the roadside path, in company with the Midshires Way. At the end of the row of estate cottages it turns left, on a grassy track waymarked with the double acorn logo. Through a swing-gate it keeps ahead and follows to the right of the hedge across an arable field to another gate on the edge of woodland known as Harlestone Heath. From here a path runs through the trees to a main crosstracks, where the route turns left.

This part of the Althorp estate is managed for the production of timber and undergoes a more or less continuous cycle of felling and replanting. The soil is sandy and many Scots pines have been planted, which is why this area is more commonly known as Harlestone Firs. The sandy tracks make for easy, pleasant walking through a variety of wildlife habitats, which vary depending on the stage of re-afforestation.

The track keeps ahead past a recently cleared area to the right, across which can be seen the large saw-mill. The track bends right, now with newly planted saplings on the left, and continues to a T-junction where the route turns left. After about 50 yards, it turns right, and keeps ahead over a crosstracks as it runs through an area of mature chestnut trees and passes the sawmill on the right. After a clearing, it bears right, just before another crosstracks is reached, and turns left at the next junction. From here the track is followed to a Y-junction with the main ride or track, along which it turns left. Mature beech trees grow in this last section and the woods are finally left where a path continues ahead past a felled tree trunk.

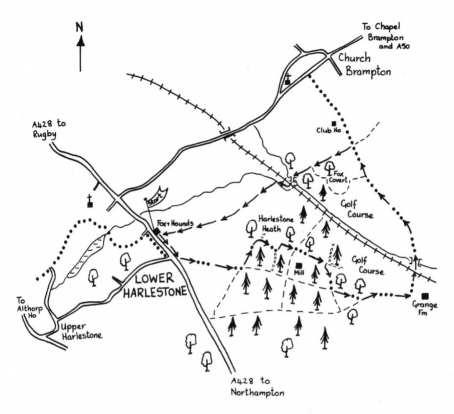

Horse-chestnut trees overhang this sandy path which runs past the end of a golf course. Eventually, it turns left, in front of Grange Farm, beyond which the outskirts of Northampton can be seen. From here the path runs down to and under a railway bridge. On the other side a good track runs across a stream and through the golf course – keep an eye open for golfers and/or golf balls! The track continues ahead up rising ground with good views on both sides as higher ground is gained. Some distance further on, a hedged-in track is followed for 100 yards or so where the pub walk turns left, and leaves the Midshires Way.

Over the stile and clear of the bushes and trees, the path runs straight across the main fairway of Church Brampton golf course with the club house at the top of the fairway to the right. Over another stile, it continues in the same direction as it runs downhill, just inside the edge of Fox Covert, from which it emerges to cross a footbridge over a stream. The path then turns left, across the end of a field, and goes back under the railway, beyond which it turns right, parallel with the embankment. Through a gate on the left towards the end of this narrow field a track runs over arable farmland across which the pub and the outskirts of Lower Harlestone soon come into view. The track keeps ahead and, after passing through several more gates, arrives back at the rear of the Fox and Hounds.

The Midshires Way – Lower Harlestone to Brixworth (6 miles)

From Lower Harlestone, the route is described in detail to just short of the Bramptom golf course club house (see above). From here a track continues to the road in the centre of Church Brampton. Here, it turns right and follows the road through Chapel Brampton, across the A50, 1 mile beyond which it turns left, through the car park of the Brampton Halt pub, down to join the Brampton Valley Way. Here what was once Pitsford and Brampton Station has been restored by the Northampton and Lamport Railway Preservation Society who operate locomotives on a reinstated stretch of line. (Overnight camping in the field behind the station is possible with prior arrangement, telephone: 01604 820327.) Walkers follow the line of the old railway almost due north to Merry Tom Crossing, where the riders' route comes in from the left. From this crossing, the route is described in Pub Walk 17 from the George, Brixworth.

[17] Brixworth
The George

Brixworth is best known for the church of All Saints, one of the oldest and best preserved Saxon churches in all Europe. However, there is much else of interest at its centre and the village is well served for hostelries, with three pubs, plus a licensed restaurant.

The George is a large, rambling building, the older part of which dwarfs later extensions built to accommodate two bars. A local whose popularity extends well beyond the village, it serves home-made pub grub at very reasonable prices. The menu cover displays a photograph of the landlord in a ring, as a reminder of his days as a professional wrestler, whilst the menu itself is divided into 'Bouts'. First Bout includes starters, such as home-made soup of the day, Second Bout is a snackweight contest, Third is for children, Fourth (the main event) has such dishes as ¼ lb locally made beefburgers with trimmings under the title of 'The Hungry Destroyer'. Due to its reputation throughout this part of the county for a well-kept pint, the pub does a roaring drinks trade, which means that meals are available at lunchtimes only, and not at all on a Sunday. There is a patio area and a barbecue at weekends during the summer. Dogs are not allowed in the bars.

The George is a Charles Wells house and serves their Eagle IPA,

Bombardier Best Bitter, and Wells Fargo, plus two guest beers, Hook Norton Old Hooky, and Young's Special. Guinness, two lagers and cider are also available on draught.

The opening times are Monday to Saturday from 11 am to 3 pm and 5.30 pm to 11 pm, and on Sunday from noon to 3 pm and 7 pm to 10.30 pm.

Telephone: 01604 881439.

How to get there: Brixworth is just off the A508, 6 miles north of Northampton. Turn off the A508 (Northampton to Market Harborough) and head for the centre. The pub is on the corner of Newlands and Harborough road, opposite the Co-op.

Parking: There is a large car park to the rear of the pub.

Length of the walk: 5½ miles (shorter and longer options possible). Map: OS Landranger 141 Kettering, Corby and surrounding area (inn GR 748707).

A walk with something for everyone, from Brixworth Country Park and Pitsford Reservoir, to restored railway locomotives. Return is via a stretch of the Brampton Valley Way and the walk culminates in a chance to view a famous Saxon church.

The Walk

From the front of the George, the route crosses over the main road to follow the no-through road opposite between the parish hall and the Co-op. It then turns left, along Holcot Road then right, on a fenced path past the end of the workshops of Holdenby Designs. The path keeps ahead between houses and across two estate roads and, clear of the houses, follows the hedge down to stiles each side of the A508 bypass.

From here there are good views of Pitsford Reservoir in the valley below and, over the road, the path enters Brixworth Country Park which surrounds the lower half of the reservoir. A wide, grassy track runs downhill to a stile and track just short of the foreshore. This track could be used to circumnavigate the reservoir, however, the pub walk turns right and, over another stile, runs through a small car park reserved for anglers.

The reservoir, known as Pitsford Water, is one of the most popular game fisheries in the Midlands. Regularly stocked with good quality brown and rainbow trout, fishing is by fly only. For details, telephone: 01604 781350.

Past the car park the track skirts the Sailing Club's dinghy park and emerges on an access road to the front of the club house. To the left is

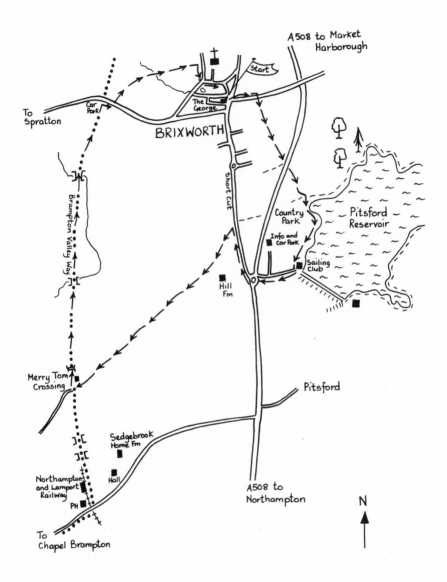

A508 to Market Harborough

To Spratton

Car Park

The George

BRIXWORTH

Start

Short Cut

Brampton Valley Way

Country Park

Info and Car Park

Sailing Club

Pitsford Reservoir

Hill Fm

Merry Tom Crossing

Pitsford

Sedgebrook Home Fm

Northampton and Lamport Railway

Hall

PH

A508 to Northampton

To Chapel Brampton

N

the reservoir dam, the length of which is open to walkers. Here, the walk turns right, and keeps ahead on the access road past a turning on the right leading to Brixworth Country Park Visitors' Centre (open Sundays).

At the roundabout, the route crosses back over the A508 and turns right along the Brixworth road. A roadside path is followed past the entrance to Hill Farm Manor House and a short-cut can be taken by staying with the road which runs directly back to the pub. The main walk, however, turns left, on a stony track signposted 'Merry Tom and Brampton Valley Way'.

Clear of the farm buildings the track first runs downhill with good views across the valley towards the distant village of Spratton. Up a rise, the track is followed by overhead electricity lines as it runs down and past an isolated house to Merry Tom Crossing on the Brampton Valley/Midshires Way. Here the main walk turns right, along the dismantled railway line, but, for those with the time and the energy, by turning left the Brampton Valley Way can be followed back to Brampton Halt. Here, what was once Pitsford and Brampton Station has been restored by the Northampton and Lamport Railway Preservation Society who operate locomotives on a reinstated stretch of line. (Overnight camping in the field behind the station is possible with prior arrangement, telephone: 01604 820327.)

Having turned right at Merry Tom Crossing, named after a favourite hunter belonging to an earlier Earl Spencer, the walk follows the old railway line, now designated as a linear Country Park. Wildlife flourishes along the embankments and cuttings in which flowers attract butterflies in the summer months, whilst birds such as woodpeckers and tree-creepers can be seen in the woodlands, spinneys and shady areas. Under a bridge, the track runs almost due north for 1 mile. Two substantial bridges over streams are crossed before reaching the car park and picnic site at Spratton Road Crossing, where the pub walk leaves the Brampton Valley/Midshires Way.

Here, the walk turns right, along the road for 50 yards or so. At a fingerpost it turns left, along a footpath across an arable field, aiming roughly left of the distant church spire. On the far side of the field a stone stile is crossed, and the path keeps to the left of a small stream. Where the hedge ends, it bears left, across open pasture. Over another stile and stream, the path continues up rising ground, aiming now directly for the church spire. After several more stiles and pastures, the path passes through a gap to the left of a dry-stone wall; the wall is followed to the corner of the field. Over a last stile a fenced path leads past two new houses and follows a drive to a road, where the route turns left, up to a junction. From here, the route bears right, along a road which runs back to the centre of the village. A hundred yards or so along the road, opposite the remains of an ancient cross, a narrow lane leads up to All Saints' church, one of the best preserved Saxon churches in the country. Detailed guides to the church and the village of Brixworth are on sale inside the church.

At the road junction the route turns right, along the High Street, and right again, opposite the Coach and Horses. From here the road leads past the Red Lion, back to the George.

Midshires Way – Brixworth to Maidwell (4 miles)
From Merry Tom Crossing the route continues along the Brampton Valley Way and is described in detail as far as Spratton Road Crossing (see above). From here it stays with the dismantled railway line and, at the next crossing, passes the site of Brixworth Station, behind which are located the Pytchley Hunt kennels and stables. A mile or so further on, Houghton Crossing is reached, beyond which the route is described in Pub Walk 18 from the Stag's Head, Maidwell.

[18] Maidwell
The Stag's Head

Maidwell is a small village which, in spite of its size, once had two churches and two manor houses. Today, only one church survives, to the east of the main road (A508), behind which the remaining manor house, Maidwell Hall, is now a well-known boys' school.

The Stag's Head has long been associated with the local hunt, which still meets there once a year. A long building built of local stone, its recorded use as a pub dates back to 1766 when it was known as the Goat. Bed and breakfast accommodation is available and separate public and lounge bars are furnished and decorated in a traditional style. A gleaming collection of brasses sets off the dark beams and exposed stonework, whilst off the cosy lounge with its open fireplace is a spacious dining-room. Blackboards display bar meals which range from giant Yorkshire puds with chunky steak to oriental specials, whilst the restaurant menu includes such dishes as venison in red wine and black cherry sauce, or pork in Madeira and cider sauce. There is always a selection of vegetarian dishes, and children are catered for. In the large garden behind the pub a permanent barbecue operates during the summer months.

The Stag's Head is a freehouse with a good choice of real ales, including Morland Old Speckled Hen, Ruddles County, Courage Directors, Webster's Yorkshire Bitter and Wadworth 6X. Guinness, three lagers and two ciders are also available on draught.

The opening times are Monday to Saturday 11 am to 2.30 pm and 5.30 pm to 11 pm and on Sunday 12 noon to 3 pm and 7 pm to 10.30 pm.

Telephone: 01604 686219.

How to get there: Maidwell is on the main A508 (Northampton to Market Harborough) road, 6 miles south of Market Harborough and only 1 mile south of the A1/M1 link road, the A14(T). The pub is on the main road, near the centre of the village.

Parking: There is a large car park to one side of the pub.

Length of the walk: 6 miles (shorter or longer options possible). Map: OS Landranger 141 Kettering, Corby and surrounding area (inn GR 746770).

A walk that first heads south along good tracks, with wide views down the Brampton Valley. The more energetic have a choice of extending the walk to visit Cottesbrooke Hall and/or Lamport Hall, whilst the return leg provides easy walking along the Brampton Valley Way, a linear park along a dismantled railway line.

The Walk

From the Stag's Head the route turns right, along the roadside path down to a crossroads, where it turns right again, along a no through lane. At a junction it keeps left, past Hall Farm, after which it bears right, up and over rising ground. Along this stretch there are the first good views across rolling farmland after which the track runs down and over a patch of low-lying woodland. Beyond this, the route keeps left at the fork to Dale Farm and the track climbs back up to higher ground with more views to the south down the length of the valley. Ahead can be seen the distant buildings of Blueberry Lodge Farm. Much of the land surrounding this farm is now set-aside, a change which has obviously benefited local wildlife since the farmer reports that, for the first time in many years, the barn owls are back!

When the farm is reached, a short-cut can be taken which turns left, down the side of the first barn on that side, and follows a track across to the Brampton Valley Way (see map).

The route of the main pub walk, however, continues ahead, past the white farmhouse. The track now becomes more of a headland path as it crosses open fields, keeping first to one side of the hedge, then the other. At the now derelict buildings of Blueberry Grange, the main route

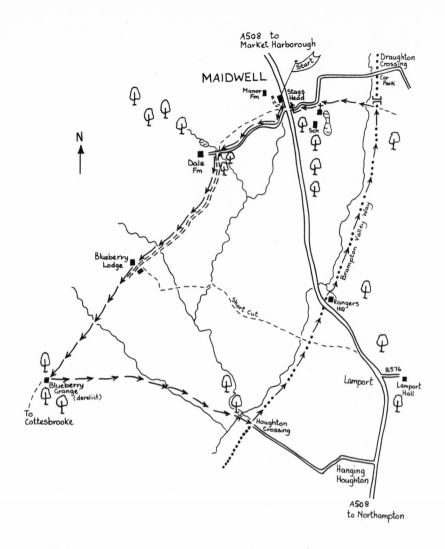

turns left, down the side of the old barn past which it bears sharply left, heading east across the valley.

(Those wishing to visit Cottesbrooke Hall should keep ahead along the track past Blueberry Grange, and turn right, along the road into the village. The Hall is open afternoons on Thursdays and bank holidays, from April to September. Telephone: 01601 24808.

Having turned left, the pub walk stays with a track over wide, arable fields and crosses over two streams before meeting the Brampton Valley/Midshires Way at Houghton Crossing.

At Houghton Crossing the way turns left, and follows the dismantled railway line. The constant change from shallow cutting to elevated embankment provides an ever changing source of interest and the walking is relaxed and easy. Just before a road is reached, a bridletrack crossing from left to right marks where the short-cut rejoins the main walk.

(Those who wish to visit Lamport Hall can turn right, along the bridletrack which leads up to the road just outside the village. Lamport Hall is open on Sunday afternoons and bank holidays, Easter to the end of September. Also on Thursday afternoons during July and August. Telephone: 01601 28272.) Over the A508 at Lamport Crossing, the walk continues past the site of the old station and the station house, now used as the headquarters of the Brampton Valley Countryside Project and workbase for Countryside Rangers. Past here, the path dog-legs ahead across a new bridge over a shallow stream, and continues along the valley over open farmland. Eventually, an overhead iron footbridge is reached, in front of which the pub walk leaves the Midshires Way.

Just before the bridge, the walk turns left, over a stile, on a footpath signposted to Maidwell village. Over a narrow pasture the path crosses a footbridge and then keeps to the left of the hedge, up a long field. Through a gate in the top corner, a short track leads to a road along which the route turns left. Past the church in front of Maidwell Hall School, and through the attractive, older part of the village, it meets the main A508. Here it turns right, back up to the Stag's Head.

Midshires Way – Maidwell to Great Oxendon (3½ miles)

From Houghton Crossing the route continues along the Brampton Valley Way and is described in detail as far as the iron footbridge (see above). From here it continues along the line of the dismantled railway and over Draughton Crossing. Above Green Lane Crossing the track runs under the new A14(T) where the riders' route turns off to the right. Walkers, however, stay with the track through the first of two tunnels (400 metres), before crossing the road next to a car park where Kelmarsh Station once stood next to the Kelmarsh Arms. Just over 1 mile further on it goes over another crossing, and from here the route is described in Pub Walk 19 from the George, Great Oxendon.

[19] Great Oxendon
The George

Great Oxendon is built on high ground from which it is said that seven hunting counties can be seen and counted. The George has been an inn since the 16th century and its current popularity is entirely due to the proprietor who, as a QE2 trained chef, 'runs a tight ship' and maintains the highest standards. En-suite bedrooms provide accommodation in a new, purpose built wing overlooking the gardens. A conservatory off the very comfortable lounge provides a light and airy dining area for bar meals. To the front of the pub three linked, semi open-plan rooms create a stylish restaurant. The inn is renowned for its fine cuisine in which the emphasis is on fresh, local produce. Beef and Guinness pie or fresh grilled haddock are typical bar meals, whilst the Victorian style restaurant serves such superb dishes as smoked salmon and trout platter or noisettes of lamb with Madeira sauce. A vegetarian choice is always available and a traditional roast lunch is served on Sundays. Meals are not available on a Sunday evening, when the pub is shut. There is a patio behind the conservatory which overlooks a very pleasant and typically English garden. Dogs are welcome in the garden, muddy boots in the bar or restaurant are not.

The George is a freehouse and serves Adnams Bitter, and Worthington

Draught Bass. John Smith's Bitter, Guinness, two lagers and cider are also available on draught.

The opening times are Monday to Saturday from 11.30 am to 3 pm and 6.30 pm to 11 pm, and on Sunday from 12 noon to 3 pm only. Telephone: 01858 465205.

How to get there: Great Oxendon is 2 miles south of Market Harborough, on the A508 to Northampton, and 2 miles north of the A1/M1 link road, the A14(T). The pub is on the A508.

Parking: There is a large car park to one side of the pub.

Length of the walk: 4¹/₂ miles. Map: OS Landranger 141 Kettering, Corby and surrounding area (inn GR 736834).

A walk to Arthingworth which incorporates a stretch of the Jurassic Way, the county's newest long-distance footpath. However, for many its most memorable feature will come just before the end, when a dismantled railway line, now designated the Brampton Valley Way, is followed through a long tunnel.

The Walk

From the George the route turns right, along the roadside path to where the recently opened Jurassic Way crosses from left to right. Here, the walk turns right, along the drive to Tunnels End, then left, over a stile, on a path signposted to Braybrooke. From here the path heads diagonally left, across small pastures and stiles to the rear of some farm buildings. Over another stile, the path leads through trees at the top of a railway cutting to a T-junction, where the route turns right, along the combined Jurassic/Midshires Way.

After crossing the top end of the tunnel, another stile takes the path clear of the trees, then down and up a wide pasture, on the other side of which it crosses double stiles. From here the path heads left, across the bottom corner of a field, and continues in the same direction, over more stiles, before bearing right, up to the corner of Waterloo Lodge. Here it turns left, over a stile, then right, along a fence. At the corner another stile is crossed and the path clears the buildings as it follows the hedge down to the bottom of a small valley. Past a pond a stile is crossed and the route keeps ahead up and over a wide, arable field to another stile next to a track, where the pub walk leaves the Midshires Way walkers' route.

Along the valley to the left can be seen the church spire of the distant village of Braybrooke. The pub walk, however, turns right, and follows the track up to the road running along the ridge. Over the road at the

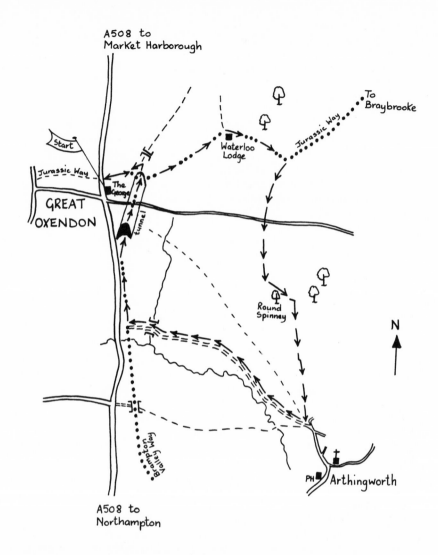

A508 to
Market Harborough

Start

Jurassic Way

GREAT
OXENDON

The George

tunnel

Waterloo
Lodge

Jurassic Way

To
Braybrooke

Round
Spinney

N

Brampton
Valley Way

A508 to
Northampton

PH Arthingworth

highest point for miles around, there are good views to the south as a
footpath is followed diagonally left, down a wide pasture. At the bottom
corner, it forks left, through a gap in the hedge and continues to run
downhill, keeping to the left of the clump of trees known as Round
Spinney. At the bottom right-hand corner, it turns right, keeping to the
right of the hedge before switching to the other side via a footbridge at
a gap in the hedge. In the next corner, a metal gate and a short track
leads to a road on the outskirts of Arthingworth. The road to the left

leads into the village, but the pub walk turns right, on a 'no-through' tarmaced track running north-westerly across the Brampton Valley. The track crosses wide, flat pastures, most of which are set-aside and used for grazing horses. After about half a mile of easy walking, it meets the dismantled railway line of the Brampton Valley Way.

Here, the walk joins the long-distance route as it turns right, along the dismantled railway line. The banks of the cutting on either side gradually get higher and steeper as the line approaches the ridge crossed earlier and, eventually, the tunnel entrance is reached. The tunnel is 440 metres long, but feels longer, and a torch is a great help in avoiding the occasional puddles where water seeps and drips from above. A ventilation shaft halfway through gives a dim light, but this only serves to heighten the overall blackness. Weird echoes accompany progress through the tunnel but the only real danger is from the ladies, as they have a tendency to hang on tightly with both hands!

Out of the tunnel, the track is followed as far as an overhead bridge. Just before the bridge the walk leaves the Brampton Valley Way as it turns left, up steps in the embankment waymarked with the double acorn logo of the Midshires Way. The path doubles back through trees along the top of the embankment and, after a short distance, meets the path to the right above the tunnel entrance used on the outward leg. Here, the pub walk turns right and leaves the Midshires Way for the second time.

From the tunnel, the route is retraced, back to the George.

Midshires Way – Great Oxendon to Sutton Bassett (6 miles)

From the crossing before the Great Oxendon tunnel, the route at first stays with the Brampton Valley Way and is described in the second section above. From the tunnel it leaves the Brampton Valley Way and is described in the first section which takes it past Waterloo Lodge (see above). Here the route turns left, on a track into Braybrooke. At a crossroads in the village, it turns right, on the Desborough road off which it turns left, on a footpath. Under the railway it first crosses a field and then a road to take a path from the yard of Braybrooke Lodge. Across three fields it dog-legs right, across the A6, and follows a lane off which a footpath on the right eventually becomes a bridleway leading to Red Hovel. Here, the route turns right, along the lane and, just before Brampton Ash, it turns left, on a footpath round the back of the village. Across the A427, it turns left, then right, on a bridletrack running north. Through a series of gates it climbs to the top of the ridge and eventually arrives at a junction known as the Five Ways. From here the route is described in Pub Walk 20 from the Queen's Head, Sutton Bassett.

[20] Sutton Bassett
The Queen's Head Inn

Sutton Bassett lies just inside the Northamptonshire border, situated on a ridge from which there are extensive views across the Welland Valley and surrounding countryside. The Queen's Head stands on the road next to a white building on which a plaque commemorates Queen Victoria and her reign. Inside, the pub consists of two, open-plan bars, one at the front of the building and another to the rear. Simply but comfortably furnished, they both have log fires, whilst the entrance between the two has an array of copper pans as more than a hint that this is a food oriented establishment. The inn has built up a deservedly high reputation for the quality and variety of its home cooking, with customers travelling many miles to sample such dishes as chicken Mississippi, (breast of chicken, cooked in garlic butter, mushrooms, cream and Southern Comfort), or the local trout Cleopatra, (trout pan-fried in butter with prawns and capers). More traditional favourites include a choice of home-made pies or Cumberland sausage. On Fridays and weekends the pretty, upstairs restaurant opens to cope with the heavy demand. This makes booking in advance, especially for Sunday lunch, virtually essential. A choice of vegetarian dishes is always available and meals are served throughout the week. To the rear of the inn, a terraced area provides an ideal vantage point for wide views across the valley to the west.

The Queen's Head is a freehouse and serves a good selection of real ales, including Marston's Queen's Head, Adnams Bitter, Worthington Draught Bass, Greene King Abbot Ale, Hop Back Wheat Beer, Butcombe Bitter, Shepherd Neame Spitfire Ale, and Thomas Caffrey Irish Ale. The choice of real ales is constantly changing and a blackboard advertises 'Forthcoming Attractions'. Guinness and cider are also available on draught.

The opening times are Monday to Saturday 11.45 am to 2.30 pm and 6.30 pm to 11 pm, and on Sunday from 12 noon to 3 pm and 7 pm to 10.30 pm.

Telephone: 01858 463530.

How to get there: Sutton Bassett lies just inside the Northamptonshire/ Leicestershire border, only 2¹/₂ miles north-east of Market Harborough. The pub is at the centre of the hamlet on the B664, which turns off the A427 (Market Harborough to Corby).

Parking: There is a car park to the rear of the inn.

Length of the walk: 3¹/₂ miles (shorter option possible). Map: OS Landranger 141 Kettering, Corby and surrounding area (inn GR 771902).

A walk with panoramic views across the Welland Valley and into Leicestershire. Down in the valley the wooden bridge across the river Welland marks not only the border, but also a final parting with the Midshires Way.

The Walk

From the Queen's Head the route turns left, past Old Chapel Cottage and, further along, All Saints' church with its 13th century bell-cote. After the houses end, the road continues uphill and, at the top, the route turns right, on a bridleway track running along the ridge. Just past an Anglian water facility on the left stands the red-brick and reinforced concrete remains of a Second World War Royal Observer Corps look-out post. Sited here to take advantage of the panoramic views across the surrounding countryside, it was once part of an early warning system meant to protect Midlands' industry and cities such as Coventry. How dismal, dark and lonely the blacked-out nights must have been up here, with only the wind and wail of distant sirens for company!

Past the old look-out post and a derelict cottage, a gate next to a small pond gives access to hilltop sheep pastures. From here the path runs ahead, keeping to the left of the hedge. Past the end of a barn on the

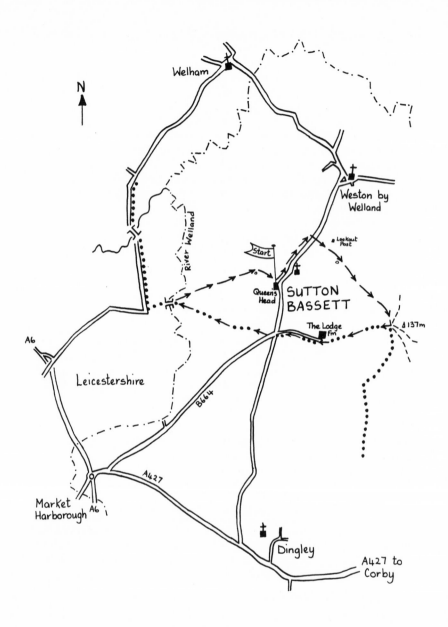

N

Welham

Weston by
Welland

River Welland

Look out
Post

Start

Queens
Head

SUTTON
BASSETT

△137m

The Lodge
Fm

A6

Leicestershire

B664

A427

Market
Harborough A6

Dingley

A427 to
Corby

right, it continues between electricity pylons to the corner of the field and through another gate. Across another field in which the outlines of ancient ridge and furrow ploughing can be seen, a third gate takes the path past another small pond and along the edge of an arable field to a cross track known as the Five Ways, where the pub walk joins the Midshires Way.

Here, the highest point in the area, the walk turns right, through another gate. There are good all-round views as the path follows the hedge downhill, aiming for the distant farm buildings in the bottom of the valley. Several gates now take the route through the farmyard belonging to Lodge Farm, on the other side of which an access road leads to the road into Sutton Bassett. At this point a short-cut can be taken by turning right, back up to the village, but the main route turns left, along the verge of the Market Harborough road. After 50 yards or so, it leaves the road as it turns right, through a gate and follows the hedge in a westerly direction across the valley. The path switches to the other side of the hedge via a gate and continues ahead over more pastures. Eventually, it arrives at a gated wooden bridge over the river Welland, on the Northamptonshire/Leicestershire border where the pub walk leaves the Midshires Way for the last time.

Just short of the bridge, the walk turns right, through another field gate. The route now heads across a first, wide pasture aiming for the village on the ridge ahead. Through double gates the hedge is followed up rising ground as far as a large willow tree to the left of a small pond. Here the path angles right, and runs up the hill, at the top of which it arrives just to the left of the Queen's Head.

The Midshires Way – Sutton Bassett northwards

From the Five Ways Crossing the route is described in detail as far as the wooden bridge on the county border (see above). Across the wooden bridge over the river Welland, the Midshires Way continues northwards for over 130 miles through the counties of Leicestershire, Nottinghamshire, Derbyshire and into Greater Manchester, where it links up with the Trans Pennine National Trail. Pub walks along the long-distance path through these counties will be described in a future guide to the northern half of the route.

The Midshires Way
Information and accommodation

BUCKINGHAMSHIRE
Tourist Information Centres
Wendover – The Clock Tower, High Street. Tel: 01296 696759.
Buckingham – The Old Gaol Museum, Market Hill. Tel: 01280 823020.
Milton Keynes – 411 Secklow Gate East. Tel: 01908 232525/231742.
Accommodation
North Bucks Way:
Great Kimble – The Bernard Arms. Tel: 01844 346172/3.
Waddesdon – The Five Arrows Hotel. Tel: 01296 651727.
Quainton – The White Hart. Tel: 01296 655234.
Winslow – The Bell Hotel. Tel: 01296 712741/714091.
Great Horwood – Grange Stables. Tel: 01296 712051.
Whaddon – The Lowndes Arms. Tel: 01908 501706.
The Swan's Way:
Loughton, Milton Keynes – The Corner House. Tel: 01908 605321.
Milton Keynes – Y.H.A. Tel: 01908 310944.
Tathall End – Woad Farm. Tel: 01908 510985.

NORTHAMPTONSHIRE
Tourist Information Centres
Northampton – Visitors' Centre, 10 St Giles Square. Tel: 01604 226677.
Market Harborough – Adam and Eve Street. Tel: 01858 468106.
Kettering – The Coach House, Sheep Street. Tel: 01536 410266.
Corby – Civic Centre, George Street. Tel: 01536 407507.
Accommodation
Quinton Green – Quinton Green Farm. Tel: 01604 863685.
Grand Union canal:
Blisworth – Blisworth Hotel. Tel: 01604 859551.
Nether Heyford – 27 Church Street. Tel: 01327 340872.
Brampton Valley Way:
Maidwell – The Stag's Head. Tel: 01604 686219.
Great Oxendon – The George. Tel: 01858 465205.
Camping
Blisworth – The Royal Oak. Tel: 01604 858372.
Chapel Brampton – Brampton Halt, Northampton and Lamport
Railway. Tel: 01604 820327.